Never Broke Again, Passive Income Trends:

25 Simple Steps to Financial Freedom

Table of Contents

CHAPTER I: YOUTUBE CHANNEL 5

CHAPTER II: AFFILIATE MARKETING 11

CHAPTER III: DIGITAL CONTENT 23

CHAPTER IV: FICTION or NON-FICTION BOOKS 27

CHAPTER V: LOW-CONTENT BOOKS 33

CHAPTER VI: MAGAZINE PUBLISHING 41

CHAPTER VII: DIGITAL MARKETING 47

CHAPTER VIII: SOCIAL MEDIA INFLUENCER 53

CHAPTER VIIII: PODCASTING 57

CHAPTER X: BLOGGING 61

CHAPTER XI: MUSIC DISTRIBUTION 69

CHAPTER XII: DOMAIN FLIPPING 73

CHAPTER XIII: STOCK PHOTOS 81

CHAPTER XIIII: DROPSHIPPING 85

CHAPTER XV: PRINT ON DEMAND 93

CHAPTER XVI: VENDING MACHINES 99

CHAPTER XVII: ATMs 103

CHAPTER XVIII: REAL ESTATE 109

CHAPTER XVIIII: ANGEL INVESTING 115

CHAPTER XX: DIVIDEND STOCKS 117

CHAPTER XXI: COMPOUND INTEREST INVESTMENTS 119

CHAPTER XXII: PASSIVELY INVESTS IN THE MARKETS 121

CHAPTER XXIII: HIGH-YIELD SAVINGS ACCOUNTS 123

CHAPTER XXIIII: LIFE INSURANCE 129

CHAPTER XXV: CREATE AN APP 133

Introduction

Are you tired of struggling to make ends meet? Ready to achieve financial freedom?

If so, then it's time to start thinking about generating passive income. Generating passive income has become increasingly popular among entrepreneurs, freelancers, and anyone looking to make a steady income without working full-time. But what exactly is passive income? What are some of the most common methods for creating it? And how long does it take to build up enough passive income to live off of?

The need or desire many people have to become financially independent has been around as long as money itself. It is a dream shared by millions of people worldwide, and it has steadily gained more and more traction in recent years. With the rise of digital technologies, the internet, and mobile apps, the potential to make money without having to work hard or long hours has become much more achievable.

This book is designed to help you understand passive income, how it works, and how you can start generating it yourself. It will provide a comprehensive overview of 25 ways to generate passive income and include tools, resources, websites, software, and apps commonly used in these methods. In addition, this book will cover the process and method of achieving passive income and the time it takes to build up enough of an income stream that may allow you to live off of it.

Whether you're just starting with passive income or have been working on it for some time now, this book will provide the information and resources you need to achieve financial freedom.

It's time to build an income stream that works for you, not against you. Let's get started!

How to use this book AS YOUR TOOLKIT

This book will help you build a successful and profitable passive income stream. It will guide you on the steps needed to get started, create multiple income streams, and ultimately begin living off your passive income.

Throughout this book, you will learn the following:

- Different types of passive income streams
- How to generate passive income quickly and easily
- Tools, resources, websites, software and apps commonly used to gain passive income
- And much more!

By reading these 25 ways to generate passive income and following the steps outlined in each section, you'll be well on your way toward achieving financial freedom.

CHAPTER I

YOUTUBE CHANNEL

Typically, when people think about YouTube, they picture a place to learn something new or kill time by watching music videos. However, another set of people anticipates YouTube to be an essential contributor to the success of their online enterprise.

Although making money on YouTube does take some time and work, the rewards can be substantial and long-term. All you have to do is devise a creative idea and execute it in an organized manner. There are several different ways to make money on YouTube. Still, the main ones are ads appearing on your videos (Google Adsense), setting up affiliate links, or selling merchandise related to your YouTube channel.

When it comes to passive income, YouTube is a desirable option. All you have to do once your channel is set up and running is upload new content regularly, monitor the viewership and interaction with your audience, and collect payments for ad revenue or affiliate links.

If you want to establish a steady stream of passive income through your YouTube channel, choose a topic you are passionate about and can offer unique insights on. Once you have identified your niche, create engaging content that will keep viewers coming back for more and attract new followers. Most importantly, be patient and consistent in your efforts – it takes time to build a successful YouTube channel!

Here are some helpful tips to get you started:

Niche down:

Choose a niche that you are passionate about and have some knowledge of. If you want to make a significant impact, narrow your focus and select a topic that will be easy to compete in.

Do keyword research:

Ensure that your content is something people desire – contemplate what words you would type in to discover those videos, and include them as such.

Use a SEO-friendly format:

Organize your content in a search engine-optimized way, using a descriptive title for each video while also including appropriate tags and keywords.

Interact with your audience:

Make sure you are responding to comments and questions posted by your viewers. Spend time engaging with them. This helps to build a stronger relationship and trust between you and your audience.

Be consistent:

Consistency is vital when it comes to YouTube success. Try to set a schedule of uploading videos on specific days and times so that your followers know when to expect new content.

CREATE A YOUTUBE ACCOUNT

You must sign up for a YouTube channel before you can start making money with the platform. Google owns YouTube. Therefore, you must use a Gmail address to sign up. After signing up for a YouTube account and activating it, it's time to start uploading videos to your channel.

Even if you create an account, you may still need to be eligible to make money. Two of YouTube's requirements for account holders are building an audience and keeping activity at a certain level. Attracting a sizable audience demonstrates that your channel is worthy of monetization.

MAKE VIDEOS

YouTube creators who want to attract and grow their audiences must consistently produce material that users want to watch. Therefore, making videos is the next logical step. However, there is no one-size-fits-all formula for determining success or failure on YouTube. Video content, such as music videos and home movies shot on smartphones have proven to be particularly popular.

Most smartphones these days include high-resolution cameras, making their use practical and efficient. If you want a high-definition (HD) recording, crank up your phone's video recording settings to the max. Then, use a DSLR camera and an external microphone for an even more polished end product.

You can use a free desktop application like Windows Movie Maker or iMovie or a premium program like Adobe Premiere, which has more advanced options. You can use YouTube's free, rudimentary editor to create and modify videos. Make sure that no protected songs are used in the final cut of your video. Your films will be removed from YouTube's ad rotation if so.

UPLOAD TO YOUTUBE AND CONFIGURE FOR SEO

Putting your finished video on YouTube comes next. You can add multiple videos by dragging and dropping them into the uploader or add a single video by pressing the upload arrow. The time it takes to upload your video will vary significantly based on its size and Internet connection speed. If you don't close the upload page in your browser, you can add numerous videos simultaneously.

You can complete the form associated with your video after it has been submitted or while it is still uploading. The title, description, category, and tags you create should contain as much information as possible. Good search engine optimization (SEO) can make the difference between a few thousand views and a few million views on YouTube, the second-largest search engine in the world.

PROMOTE YOUR VIDEO

Spread the word now that your video is live on the Internet. Distribute the clip anywhere you can, including online communities, blogs, forums, and message boards. People can see your video on YouTube by linking it to or embedding it on other websites. Spamming will get you nowhere and will only hurt your video views.

Marketing your videos will bring in more viewers and potential subscribers. Your ability to monetize the material is aided by a larger audience. To make money off your videos, you need to get your channel up and to run, amass a library's worth of content, and get a dedicated viewership.

YOUTUBE PARTNER PROGRAM

Applying for YouTube's Partner Program (YPP) is the first step toward making money from a channel's content (via advertising revenue and subscriber fees) and gaining access to premium monetization tools like AdSense. To be accepted into the YPP, a YouTube channel must have at least 500 subscribers overall and three video uploads within the last 90 days plus, either 3,000 public watch hours within the last 365 days or 3 million shorts views within the last 90 days, and be in good standing with YouTube.

Acceptance into the YouTube Partner Program is required before opening an AdSense account. Google's AdSense is the primary advertising platform for all Google- and Google-affiliated sites, including YouTube. When an AdSense account is created, payment and tax identification information, such as a social security number or employer identification number (EIN), will need to be entered.

How much money you get from AdSense depends on three factors: how often your video is viewed, which advertisers choose to display their advertising on your video, and how often those ads are clicked. To a lesser extent than overall views, high levels of interaction and clicks are more indicative of success. Depending on your video's attractiveness, you can make anywhere from 30 cents to $10 per 1,000 views.

To make more money with your videos, focus on creating content that people will watch.

YOUTUBE'S OTHER MONEY-MAKING OPPORTUNITIES

SPONSORSHIP

YouTubers may monetize their material in more ways than just adverts and subscriptions. Marketers always look for influential people to help spread the word about their products and services. Since YouTube has such a large user base, it is an ideal place to showcase advertisements. In addition, advertisers may get in front of YouTube's massive audience by teaming up with channel creators through sponsorship agreements.

YouTubers can make lots of money by becoming brand sponsors and advertising for brands in their videos. Unfortunately, it's common for YouTubers to advertise the product without assurances. Sponsorship is frequently included in videos that do not promote the product.

ENDORSEMENT

Endorsements, like sponsorships, are negotiated between a third party and a popular YouTuber. A YouTuber's endorsement of a product or service differs from a purely promotional sponsorship. They give some warranty to their viewers and back up their statements about the product. The influencer is compensated monetarily for advocating a given product, brand, or business.

MERCHANDISE

Merch sales may be a lucrative side hustle for YouTube influencers with a sizable subscriber base and a large fan base. Fans can feel more emotionally connected to their favorite YouTubers when purchasing branded products like t-shirts and hats. So, beyond just watching their videos and subscribing to their channels, this is another opportunity to show your support for the influencer.

Popular YouTubers can make millions of dollars from selling stuff. However, thanks to their innovative packaging, some influencers' audience goes beyond their fan base. In turn, the YouTube channel gains additional viewers interested in purchasing merchandise.

CHAPTER II

AFFILIATE MARKETING

Affiliate Marketing is performance-based marketing in which an affiliate earns money by referring customers to a business or product. The recommending publisher receives a commission when a publication promotes a product or service from another retailer or advertiser via an affiliate link. When a customer is brought in through an affiliate's link, the merchant or advertiser will pay that partner a commission.

A sale is the typical end outcome. However, affiliate marketing opportunities will pay you for generating leads, signing customers for free trials, attracting visitors to their website, or distributing software.

Joining an affiliate program costs little, so there's no need to worry about the initial investment. If executed properly, affiliate marketing has the potential to transform your Internet side hustle into a full-fledged, highly profitable enterprise.

HOW AFFILIATE MARKETING WORKS

Promoting a good or service using one's website, podcast, or social media accounts is known as "affiliate marketing." When someone follows the affiliate's recommendation and makes a purchase, the affiliate receives a commission.

The business and the product set affiliate sales commissions. Earnings range from as little as 5% of sales to as high as 50% under special circumstances, such as when advertising a course or event. Some affiliate marketing programs offer a fixed dollar amount per sale rather than a percentage of the total.

TYPES OF AFFILIATE MARKETING

It's hard to tell if an affiliate has used the product they're pushing or if they're just in it for the cash. But, unfortunately, both situations persist to this day.

Only in 2009 did prominent affiliate marketer Pat Flynn classify affiliate marketers into three distinct categories. Learning about these forms of affiliate marketing can broaden your perspective on the industry.

UNATTACHED AFFILIATE MARKETING

In this kind of affiliate marketing effort, you promote a product without building a significant online profile or establishing yourself as an industry expert. There is no personal involvement on your part; all you're doing is using paid advertising platforms like Google Adwords or Facebook Ads to expose an affiliate link to a potential customer in hopes that they'll click on it and make a purchase, which would in turn, increase your earnings.

The fact that no physical presence or established credibility is required, it's one of the things that make this affiliate marketing model very appealing, to many.

RELATED AFFILIATE MARKETING

Related affiliate marketing is a subset of affiliate marketing that is particularly effective. For example, you have an online presence (a blog, a podcast, a video series, or a social media account), and you promote affiliate links to products in your field that you don't personally use.

You don't have to use the product yourself, but you must be in a related industry. By doing so, your audience will trust you as an authority and will be more likely to buy from you when they see you're promoting something that could help them.

INVOLVED AFFILIATE MARKETING

Involved affiliate marketing is when you recommend a product or service to your audience that you have used and believe in. Not via a banner ad or a section labeled "suggested resources," but organically as you go about your daily business and plan your approach to the topic. As a step in the procedure, the product is almost necessary.

PROS AND CONS OF AFFILIATE MARKETING

The rising interest in affiliate marketing suggests that it is worthy of pursuing. With a value of $5.4 billion in 2017, Statista predicts that the affiliate marketing sector will grow to $8.2 billion by 2023. So it's a highly lucrative business opportunity that won't break the bank. But before you jump in head first, you should weigh the benefits and drawbacks of affiliate marketing.

Pros

While expanding markets is a positive sign of success, there are other reasons why entrepreneurs choose to promote their businesses through word of mouth.

EASY TO EXECUTE

With regards to your contribution, for the most part, you just manage the product's digital marketing. The more challenging parts, like creating, maintaining, or delivering the offer, are taken care of for you.

LOW RISK

Because there is no charge to become an affiliate, you may immediately begin making money with a proven affiliate product or service. The ideal financial situation would involve an affiliate marketing strategy that generates a substantial amount of passive revenue through commission. An affiliate link can bring in consistent income, but only after you put in some work to develop traffic sources.

EASY TO SCALE

If you're doing affiliate marketing right, you can increase your earnings by a large margin without hiring more people. In addition, as your existing work keeps churning out affiliate commissions, you could expand by introducing even more products to your audience.

However, before you get too excited, remember that trustworthy relationships are the foundation of successful affiliate marketing. Even though it may feel like there's no shortage of products or services to sell, it's usually preferable to focus on the ones you've used or would recommend to others. Being a successful affiliate marketer for a product requires significant effort, even if that product piques your interest or fits neatly into an existing passion.

Cons

A few drawbacks to affiliate marketing make it less ideal than other forms of advertising. First, look at the obstacles you'll face while moving towards affiliate marketing success.

REQUIRES PATIENCE

Contrary to popular belief, affiliate marketing does not present promises of becoming rich overnight. Instead, building an audience and gaining trust is a process that takes time and persistence.

You should conduct A/B testing to determine the most effective method of reaching your target audience. It would be best to look into the most appropriate and trustworthy things to advertise. Invest time in lead-generating activities on your marketing channels, such as blogging, releasing free content on social media, conducting virtual events, and so on.

COMMISSION-BASED

As an affiliate marketer, your pay is not determined by a superior. Instead, affiliate programs pay a commission for generating leads, clicking through, or making a sale.

Corporations can temporarily monitor users' interactions with your material by placing cookies in their browsers. The payment is made once the desired task has been completed.

NO CONTROL OVER THE PROGRAM

Affiliates are obligated to follow the guidelines established by a corporation. Therefore, how you talk about and show off their products must adhere to their strict criteria. Your rivals will likely adopt these suggestions, so you must go outside the box to stand out.

HOW AFFILIATE MARKETERS MAKE MONEY

The range of possible earnings through affiliate marketing is quite broad. Affiliate marketers can earn anywhere from a few hundred dollars a month to six figures a year. If you're an affiliate marketer, your earnings potential directly correlates to the size of your audience.

How, exactly, do affiliates receive their commissions? You will find a variety of affiliate commission structures to consider when selecting a program to promote. In addition, companies may refer to it by several different names, including price model, payout model, conversion type, and others.

Regardless of how it's referred, the payment model specifies the KPIs resulting in compensation. It might be a download, a purchase, or in the case of software, a register for a free trial. When promoting tangible goods, the end goal for an affiliate marketer is usually a sale.

Most programs use a " last-click attribution system," whereas the affiliate who receives the user's last click before a transaction is made is given full credit for the sale. However, there has been a shift as programs enhance their attribution models and reporting. For instance, if numerous affiliates contributed to a customer's buying decision, you may divide the profit evenly.

Affiliates typically receive compensation in five ways:

Pay per sale:

If you're working on a "pay per sale" basis, you'll get a cut of the action for every transaction you facilitate. This type of compensation structure is widely used for e-commerce offerings.

Pay per action:

Commissions are earned for specific actions, hence the term "pay per action." The flexibility of this commission structure makes it popular with affiliate programs, which may apply to various types of offerings, such as newsletter subscriptions, clicks, contact requests, form submissions, etc.

Pay per install:

Installs generated from your website traffic can result in a "pay-per-install" arrangement. Therefore, your material should encourage app and software downloads and installations.

Pay per lead:

Leads paid for on a "pay per lead" basis result in a sale or subscription. Sweepstakes, lead generation, and similar offerings frequently use this compensation technique, making it widespread. For new businesses, cost-per-lead arrangements are frequent because attracting new customers is more complex than charging an existing customer base for their products.

Pay per click:

Pay-per-click is an unusual affiliate marketing payment model in which you get paid a small amount for each click on your link. Big online retailers utilize pay-per-click (PPC) advertising to spread the word about their stores' products. Customers can browse the store's website without committing to anything. Your affiliate market will determine your earnings potential.

HOW TO START AFFILIATE MARKETING

Becoming a successful affiliate requires hard work and self-control, just like running a small business. Learn how to launch a successful affiliate marketing enterprise by following these instructions.

PICK YOUR PLATFORM AND METHOD

The first thing you need to do is choose a platform for expanding your fan base. No two, affiliate marketers use the same strategy or software. Multiple strategies exist from which you can select when developing an affiliate marketing plan:

Niche topic and review sites: Review sites that cater to a specialized audience or compare one brand's offerings to its rivals are. These are good examples. To succeed with this strategy, you'll need to provide engaging and relevant content to the review space consistently.

Digital content: Bloggers, YouTubers, and social media influencers fall within the digital content makers category. They cater to a specific demographic by producing content that speaks directly to them. To achieve this, they will gradually roll out niche products they know their audience will love. So naturally, this increases the likelihood that they'll buy, therefore increasing your affiliate commission.

Courses, events, and workshops: Instructors might benefit from incorporating affiliate partnership offerings into either of these sources.

When it comes to affiliate marketing, credibility and readership are paramount.

DECIDE YOUR NICHE AND AUDIENCE

Find a topic that interests you, and that you already know a lot about. Potential clients will see you as more credible and reliable if you come off as genuine. It is also helpful in deciding which items and labels to market.

FIND YOUR PRODUCTS

To make money as an affiliate marketer, your audience needs to agree with what you're saying. Therefore, the products you push should be ones people want. If you get this right, it could heighten your success and credibility as well, increase your audience.

Wondering where to start? Don't fret. I've got you covered. If you need help searching for suitable products or brands, numerous affiliate marketplaces exist, some of which are:

- Affiliate Future
- AvantLink
- CJ Affiliate
- ClickBank
- FlexOffers

- LinkConnector
- ShareASale

Also, check the sites of companies whose products and services you enjoy using to see whether they offer an affiliate program. Websites run by significant corporations frequently have advertisements for affiliate programs like Amazon Associates and the Shopify Affiliate Program.

Another option is to be more assertive. For example, if you come across a fantastic product, contact the creator and ask if they have an affiliate program. They may be willing to work out an arrangement with you, such as providing you with a unique discount code to distribute to your audience.

If you're a health and wellness blogger and a new workout product seller, you can get an exclusive discount by contacting them before anybody else.

Studying the fine print of any affiliate marketing program's terms of service would be best to ensure you understand and can comply with them. Some affiliate programs forbid you from purchasing pay-per-click advertising that includes the product or company's name. In addition, your affiliate link will typically have a cookie within a predetermined timeframe.

CHOOSE YOUR FIRST AFFILIATE PROGRAM

The most crucial thing to remember as you think about products to promote or explore affiliate marketplaces is that they should appeal to your current or target demographic. Think about whether or not it would be helpful to your intended audience. Does this fall within your area of expertise?

A blogger who specializes in cuisine probably won't push cosmetics. Instead, selling other items, like pots and pans, meal sets, gourmet supplies, and aprons, makes more sense.

Also, be sure the service or product you're promoting is a good fit for the platform you've chosen. For instance, products like furniture and clothes lend themselves effectively to image-centric channels like Instagram. On the other hand, conversion rates may be higher on longer-form media like a blog or YouTube if you're pushing more involved products like software.

TIPS FOR AFFILIATE MARKETING SUCCESS

Earnings from affiliate marketing have the potential to become passive if a sufficient amount of groundwork is laid. The quality of your evaluation will determine how well your program performs.

Personalization is key to writing a great review. Create a blog entry, social media update, Instagram Story, or video to share your journey with the world. If you're writing a review based on your experience with the product, be as objective as possible. In general, genuineness increases as one's guard drops. If others believe in you, they will likely take your suggestions.

For your affiliate marketing to be successful, you need to build trust so that your readers will follow your advice. Of course, you'll need more credibility as an affiliate to sell a $1,000 course, for example, than a $20 pair of pants, but this will vary depending on your industry and the things you're promoting.

TALK TO A PRODUCT EXPERT

You should talk to people who have already bought and used the goods or services or even the company that produces or sells them. This can give your review more substance by allowing you to tell a story to your audience.

CREATE A PRODUCT TUTORIAL

While the size of your audience is an essential factor in affiliate marketing, a tutorial on the offer is another technique to attract visitors.

People frequently use Google to look up "how to" information. This might be anything from "how to save money for college" to "how to design a laundry room." Offering a tutorial that addresses the searcher's pain point and demonstrates the product's worth will make your recommendations more meaningful and give the client more reason to buy the item you're promoting.

BUILD AN EMAIL LIST

To send out emails to interested parties, you must compile a list of their email addresses. Gathering people's contact information is a great way to stay in touch with them outside of social media. When compared to social media and other marketing channels, email has the highest conversion rate (66%) regarding purchases made as a result of receiving marketing communication.

Add value to your email list subscribers. Be sure to reply to any emails you get from them. Maintain a regular newsletter schedule and high standards. Then, every once in a while, remind subscribers to check out your affiliate links.

There has yet to be a fixed schedule for sending out these advertisements via electronic mail. If you send them frequently, people may view you as spammy and unreliable. On the other hand, monthly promotions of high-quality products will only benefit those subscribers.

FIND RELEVANT SEARCH TERMS

Promote your offer in a blog post by thinking about the search terms people might use to discover a solution to a problem like theirs. When you need assistance, Google Ads Keyword Planner is a fantastic resource.

CONSIDER YOUR ANGLE

Consider how much time and effort you should put into creating instructional or tutorial content, as this is often the stepping-stone that leads to a customer making a purchase.

If you have a product that you want to promote, whether it's tangible or digital (like software), you can film yourself using it and demonstrating how it can benefit others. For example, post a video or write up about your experience opening the package if you order something online and have it shipped, so that you can cash in on the unboxing trend.

SET YOUR DISTRIBUTION STRATEGY

Once you've finished, it's time to put it on your website and social media pages. You can launch an email marketing campaign if you have a list of subscribers. Make sure your website serves as a hub for affiliate marketing, complete with a resource page where you can provide a quick rundown of the most valuable tools.

TRY OFFERING A BONUS

Affiliate programs are promoted in some cases by providing additional incentives to buyers. For example, if a follower makes a purchase, you may offer them a free copy of your published e-book.

Customers are inclined to purchase when an incentive such as this is offered. The worth of the freebie offered, will have more of an impact on customers if they know that it is an item you often sell from your business.

INCORPORATE LEGAL ASPECTS ACCORDINGLY

Ensure your readers know that you're using affiliate links in your piece. The Federal Trade Commission, for one, mandates it. However, connecting with your audience might be facilitated, by sharing the motivation behind your affiliation.

CHAPTER III

DIGITAL CONTENT

Unless you've been living under a rock for the past 40 years, you're probably aware of the steady improvement of material and digital content in particular. People are paying attention to videos more and more as they grow in popularity. Infographics are a more efficient way to summarize data. And it's easier than ever to spread a meme online.

There's no disputing the impact of digital media. However, you can leverage it to your advantage by creating content that generates passive income. Creating digital content requires some upfront work, but once you've got the hang of it and have a portfolio available, you'll be able to earn passive income indefinitely. Here are some of the ways you can do it:

Even though this opens up excellent content marketing prospects for companies, it also necessitates that you have a well-defined course of action in mind. This is where a plan for digital material comes into play. At this point, you have laid out the steps for developing a solid digital content strategy from scratch.

COURSES

Many people are looking to learn how to do something specific and are willing to pay for it. If you have specialized knowledge in a particular field, you can create an online course detailing your expertise and market it to people interested in learning what you know.

Courses are a great way to secure passive income. You can create an online course using e-learning platforms like Udemy and Teachable. Or you can develop your standalone course website. Either way, creating an informative course that people will pay for is a great way to earn passive income from digital content.

When creating an online course, cover all the basics first. Figure out what topics you want to outline, decide on the length of each section, and map out the structure of the entire course. Once this is figured out, you can begin building your content. Keep in mind that many courses are available, so feel free to go beyond the traditional lecture format. You can also offer interactive quizzes and assessments to engage learners.

MEMBERSHIP SITES

You've created a course and have people willing to pay for it. Great! But what about, those who are interested in learning more? That's where membership sites come into play.

A membership site is an exclusive club with additional content or benefits available to members only. You will often charge a monthly fee to access the site and its contents, such as tutorials, webinars, forums, etc. Membership sites can be great for connecting like-minded individuals within your community and offering helpful resources that go beyond what you offer in your course.

When setting up a membership site, think of ways to add value since this will be key to attracting and keeping members. You'll also want to consider how much content you'll be providing, what kind of benefits members will receive, and the support available. Once your membership site is up and running, it will become a reliable source of passive income.

The more successful your membership site is, the more time and energy you'll spend maintaining it — but that can also be part of the fun! Above all else, ensure to provide as much value as possible to keep people engaged and coming back for more.

TYPE OF EARNINGS TO BE GENERATED WITH DIGITAL CONTENT

The amount of passive income you can establish with digital content varies greatly depending on how much effort and resources you are willing to put into it. However, it is possible to make a living off the income generated from digital content with consistent effort.

For example, if you are a blogger or content creator, your blog post views might generate a little money initially, but as your audience grows, so will your income potential. In addition to that, once you have created an e-book or online course, it can continue to generate profits for years to come without any additional effort.

If you're selling digital products for $250 each and have an audience of 1000, assuming a 2% conversion rate, you'll make $5,000. If you charged $100 per product, you'd make $2,000. So the more people see your digital products and the cheaper they are, the higher your potential earnings will be.

The average annual pay for a Digital Content Creator is $69,540 as of April 29, 2022. However, it is important to remember that this number can vary greatly depending on how much effort and how many resources you put into creating content.

In conclusion, digital content has the potential to generate a steady stream of passive income over time if you are willing to create quality content and promote it correctly and consistently. By leveraging the power of online platforms such as websites and social media, businesses can reach their target audience and increase the chance of generating additional cash flow.

CHAPTER IV

FICTION OR NON-FICTION BOOKS

Book writing is an excellent way to create passive income. You can write a non-fiction book about your chosen topic and offer the finished product on Amazon, Barnes & Noble, or other online retailers for people to purchase.

When we talk about fiction, we're talking about works of literature that are entirely made up. True, these tales draw inspiration from actual events and people, but they aren't meant to be finger pointing. Speculative narratives can be found in various fictional book genres, such as mystery, science fiction, fantasy, crime thriller, romance, and many more.

However, nonfiction is sometimes referred to as "the truth-telling genre," with good reason. It refers to fictional works based on actual events and chronologically tells those stories.

As one ages, their taste in reading material shifts. Younger readers, especially, gravitate toward stories in a made-up world. It's common knowledge that people with academic jobs prefer non-fiction books that focus on teaching rather than storytelling. Besides the wide variety of fiction and nonfiction genres, there are also a wide variety of book subgenres that reflect readers' wide variety of interests.

While both are common forms of imaginative writing, the two are very different from one another.

A work of fiction is wholly made up by its author. The future of a writer's work is entirely up to them. Fiction is something made up by the author's imagination. Characters, plots, and settings are the backbone of any work of fiction.

Since fiction is not based on reality, the author can express whatever idea dominating his or her consciousness. Through this writing mode, the reader is given a glimpse into the author's inner world of make-believe. Of course, the author makes up the whole thing, including the dialogue and events. When writing fiction, there are no absolute truths.

Stories in fiction never have any basis. We know that what we read in a work of fiction can never actually happen. However much a particular character in the novel may be based on a natural person, we will never meet them in real life.

Comic books, movies, TV series, novellas, and fairy tales are all common mediums for this artistic expression. There isn't necessarily a strict genre requirement for the story. But it also veers off into science fiction, fantasy, and romance in addition to action, mystery, and thriller. A good piece of fiction writing will draw you in and hold your attention with its captivating story, even if you can guess some of the twists and turns along the way. If you can't believe it, fiction is what the entertainment industry calls the "gold standard."

Let's move on to the section on nonfiction books now. This literary genre encompasses works focusing on the dissemination of information, such as those in education, journalism, and autobiography. In writing nonfiction, one should aim for clarity and brevity. Unlike fiction, nonfiction is meant to teach readers something new or expand their horizons on a specific topic. Articles from newspapers, resume, autobiographies, and textbooks fall under the nonfiction category.

Nonfiction books are often based on actual events or facts that have been carefully researched. Non-fiction writers attempt to explain real-life concepts, provide insight into a particular topic, and draw conclusions about the world around us. In addition, they create stories of their own by weaving together factual information with contextual commentary and analysis. As such, nonfiction is an invaluable source of knowledge for entertainment and educational purposes.

In conclusion, fiction and nonfiction are two very distinct forms of literature that appeal to different readers depending on their tastes in reading material. While fiction may be more entertaining and engaging for some people, non-fiction provides a wealth of knowledge about specific topics for those who prefer it over traditional novels. Both types of literature can provide hours of entertainment and enlightenment. No matter your preference, there is a book to suit every reader's needs.

E-BOOKS

E-books have become increasingly popular in the last decade. E-books are digital books that can be read on various devices, such as computers, tablets, and smartphones. These books offer readers the same content as traditional print books but with the added convenience of being available for instant download.

E-books come in two different formats: PDFs and ePubs. PDFs are static documents that retain their formatting no matter where they are viewed or printed (e.g., you can view them on a laptop and then switch to a tablet without losing any formatting). EPubs are more dynamic than PDFs because they adapt to different device sizes and resolutions, making them ideal for reading on mobile devices with small screens.

E-books are a great way to reach readers who can't find or don't have access to traditional publications. They are also typically much cheaper than print books and offer authors the opportunity to self-publish without putting out the extra expense of printing and distribution costs. Additionally, e-books don't take up any physical space, making them an excellent option for those with limited storage options.

With the rise of e-book technology, it has become easier than ever for authors to share their work with audiences all over the world. Whether you're an aspiring novelist or a seasoned writer looking to increase your fan base, considering an e-book is worth it!

PAPERBACK BOOKS

Paperback books have been around for centuries but have remained popular. Paperbacks can be found in almost any bookstore or online retailer and are often more affordable than hardcover versions.

Paperbacks consist of two components: the book itself and a protective cover. The paperback is typically thinner and lighter than its hardback counterpart due to the use of lightweight paper stock; however, this does not necessarily mean that the content contained within it is less valuable or informative.

One benefit of paperback books is that they are usually much easier to carry and store than their hardcover counterparts, making them ideal for people who take public transportation or travel frequently. In addition, because they are generally cheaper than other types of books, they often make great gifts for book lovers on a budget.

Overall, paperback books have many advantages that appeal to readers of all ages and interests. They are relatively inexpensive, easy to carry around and offer plenty of options when it comes to content. So whether you're looking for a light read or something more in-depth, you can find interesting content in the world of paperbacks!

AUDIO BOOKS

Audiobooks have quickly become a popular form of entertainment, allowing readers to listen to stories while doing other activities like exercising, commuting, or running errands. Audiobooks are available in various formats, including digital downloads, CDs, and audio cassettes.

Unlike traditional print books, audiobooks require a certain level of commitment from the reader—you must be able to concentrate on the words being spoken to appreciate what is being said fully. It also requires a certain level of focus, as you can quickly become distracted by external noises and lose track of where you are in the story.

One benefit of audiobooks is that they often provide an enriching experience for readers who may need more time or for those who lack the ability to read a physical book. Additionally, audiobooks are available in various genres, making it easier for listeners to find something that interests them.

Audiobooks are yet another source for earning passive income and can be a great way for listeners to enjoy stories without committing to print material. So whether they're looking for a suspenseful mystery or an inspiring memoir, readers can find something captivating in audiobooks!

CHAPTER V

LOW-CONTENT BOOKS

You want to publish a book but need help doing it right. Because they require so little writing ability on the author's part, books with little substance provide a simple route for virtually anyone to enter the publishing industry.

Several people today make a living by deliberately producing books with minimal content. A low-content book requires very little to no new material to be written.

These books typically showcase a collection or invite readers to do tasks within the book. Journaling, sketching, coloring, painting, and even performing activities outside the pages are all examples of such pursuits, but the possibilities are endless.

The key to producing a successful low-content book is to provide something that readers can't easily find outside the book. This could include information, activities, templates, and forms you designed. Knowing what kinds of books will entice your target audience ensures you understand their likes and needs before putting yourself out there.

WHY CREATE A LOW-CONTENT BOOK?

Despite popular belief, writing is challenging. According to some, one can either be born with a talent for writing or develop that talent through practice and experience.

Writing the next best seller that will set the world on fire is challenging. Furthermore, there are no guarantees. So, if you want to publish a book and wish to avoid hiring a ghostwriter because you can't write an actual novel, a book with little to no content may be the answer.

It's very possible to make money off books with minimal content. Since they often take up to a few days to put together and construct, the work you spend on them usually pays off immediately. No need to spend months cooped up in front of a computer, because low-content books can be written in a matter of days.

Self-publishing can reduce the printing costs for books with minimal content. This is because the low page count (often under 100) makes use of many printers' cheaper per-page rates.

If writing a book has always been your ultimate goal, and you're determined to see it through no matter what, the good news is that creating books with little to no actual content can make that goal a reality.

Now that we've defined minimal content books and discussed why you might want to write one, we can discuss some famous and successful examples.

PROFITABLE LOW-CONTENT BOOKS YOU CAN WRITE NOW

If you need more time for novel writing, try your hand at one of these easy reads. Some common ones include the following that readers enjoy:

1. GUEST BOOK

The guestbook is one common example of a book with minimal actual content. Throughout the year, there are countless opportunities for celebrations to bring people together. In cases like these, visitor books prove invaluable. In addition, a guest book is a beautiful keepsake for special occasions like weddings, birthdays, anniversaries, and holiday parties.

2. JOURNALS

Keeping a journal is an integral component of most people's routines. That's why it's so accessible to a broad audience despite its low-content level. Depending on your intended audience, there are a wide variety of journals from which to choose.

3. MUSIC COMPOSITION NOTEBOOKS

Manuscript paper is only another name for a composition notebook. That's the gear that musicians rely on when they get the muse to write some tunes. There is minimal to no content requirement for this category. Nonetheless, extra work on the cover page often pays off.

4. COLORING BOOKS

Despite the widespread complaint that the market is already flooded with coloring books or that they are too generic, it's hard to dispute that these publications are among the most recognizable and successful in their genre.

5. WORD GAMES AND CROSSWORD PUZZLES

Word games and crossword puzzle books are other popular pastimes. In addition, you can use online word game generators to lighten the load of what initially appears to be a text-heavy undertaking.

6. PLANNERS

Planners are the most time-consuming to produce low-content books. More work should be placed into creating both the interior and the cover page to increase its appeal to buyers.

Yet, compared to other publications with minimal substance, planners are considered the most eco-friendly option. This is why many authors publish their work on making niche-specific calendars. A landscape planner or a small business planner, are two examples.

7. QUOTE BOOKS

Books filled with quotes and wise words are popular since we could all use a pick-me-up every once in a while. Of course, producing a book like this requires a lot of time and effort, but it's an excellent method to disseminate a curated collection of quotes on a specific topic.

To give just a more few examples, consider publications containing motivational sayings, expressions of love, or words of wisdom for the family. These books are in high demand because of their popularity.

TIPS ON WRITING LOW-CONTENT BOOKS

You're probably prepared to begin the writing process now that you know what kinds of low-content books to consider. To help make sure your book is a hit, here are some suggestions you can use.

STOP OVERTHINKING AND STICK WITH WHAT YOU KNOW

Overthinking is common when people are engaging in an activity for the first time. One of the most important things to remember while penning a low-content book is to focus on areas in which you have expertise.

Write down the areas of expertise that you now possess. You can use this to start thinking of concepts for your low-content book.

KNOW YOUR AUDIENCE

Determining whom you intend to sell to is crucial. Your success from this creation depends on it. To that end, you might be inspired to design a calendar just for animal-friendly people.

It's a forward step in the right direction, but it may be even more effective if you target dog lovers. The only thing to watch out for is not narrowing your focus too much and ending up without any readers. Instead, target a niche audience where you can expect reasonable demand.

KEEP YOUR PRODUCT CREATION SIMPLE

Inadvertently, spending too much time brainstorming about a wide range of topics could complicate things. So to avoid that, you may streamline the process by breaking down a single issue into a series of sub-ideas. Establishing a starting point for a specific subject allows you to go in multiple directions as you adapt the initial design to suit other audiences.

Example:

- A Diary for Mothers
- A Diary for Fathers
- A Diary for Teachers

BE OPEN TO OTHER OPPORTUNITIES

No author's journey is complete after they've written a book with minimal substance. You're free to broaden your horizons and develop new abilities. Learning from others in the same field can be influential. For example, you may consider selling print-on-demand accessories with a journal, notebook, or quote book. This could expand your portfolio and likely increase revenues.

CAN I OUTSOURCE SOME TASKS?

Self-publishing authors face many challenges. But, first, realize that there will be times when you'll need to work on your own in writing, editing, cover design, and layout.

Nevertheless, if you have to, hire someone else to do it. By implementing this approach, you could still create a unique product of which you can be proud.

HIRE PRINT-ON-DEMAND SERVICES

Writers of low-content publications should be aware that not all printed copies of their books may be sold, especially if this is their first-time publishing. Therefore, a print-on-demand service is recommended.

BANK ON POTENTIALLY SUCCESSFUL IDEAS

Betting on concepts that present a possible win is the key to being successful in this sector. If you've found success with a planner aimed at working mothers, you can ride that wave of success into other markets.

ADVANTAGES OF WRITING LOW-CONTENT BOOKS

Low-content books have benefits that take time to be noticeable compared to authoring a sophisticated and text-heavy book. You can find a few examples below.

EASIER AND QUICKER TO CREATE

Reading a book with lots of text can take a long time. Some last for as long as a year or even longer. But books with little content can be read in a just few days. Moreover, because of how simple they produce, you will have a better opportunity to publish more books from which you can earn money.

CREATING HIGH-QUALITY OUTPUTS

Simple and fast preparation automatically equates to poor quality. Take time to develop something competitive enough to stand out, which will ultimately result in increased sales.

THEY CAN SERVE AS COMPANION BOOKS TO OTHER BOOKS

If you've already had a book published, a sequel with less meat on its bones could be a great idea. This could suffice as an effective strategy for books on motivation or self-improvement. In addition, many best-selling nonfiction authors have discovered that publishing a companion magazine helps increase sales of their books.

EXCELLENT GIFT IDEAS

A wonderful present for a loved one, low-content books are simpler to produce. First, personalize it down to the cover by having it explicitly designed for the recipient. But you don't have to stop there; if you want, you can tailor the entire book to a single recipient, making the gift all the more special.

THEY DON'T REQUIRE MUCH WRITING

The daunting task of creating a book has prevented many would-be authors from putting their thoughts on paper. The fact that it takes so much time to read just one book may contribute to this sensation. Yet another reason is a lack of self-assurance in one's command of the English language or ability to write effectively. To your relief, writing a book with a low word count requires minimal effort.

Low-content books may be the ideal alternative if you want to publish a book but do not consider yourself a competent writer or need more patience to work for years to develop a novel. At first, the thought of writing a book with almost little text may seem absurd. However, after you consider its potential, you will discover it is reasonable.

Now that you know more about low-content books, the abundance of potential markets should not come as a surprise. Writing a book with minimal content might appear a bit time-consuming, but the results are well worth the effort.

Furthermore, you can use this as a springboard to launch the next phase of your writing career. For example, if you want to write a novel someday, publishing a diary or other book will help you gain the experience necessary to succeed.

CHAPTER VI

MAGAZINE PUBLISHING

When you think of passive income, magazine publishing may not immediately come to mind as an option. But if you're passionate about a specific topic (or topics), you can use your knowledge and enthusiasm to create a quarterly or monthly magazine that readers will love.

This type of passive income requires some initial effort to create the content for the first few issues, design a website, sign up for advertising services such as Google AdSense or Mediavine, and then promote your magazine through social media and other channels to attract subscribers. However, after all of the pertinent steps have been followed, it's possible to earn a steady stream of passive income from your magazine on a monthly basis.

Not only can you earn money directly from subscription fees, but you can also generate revenue through ads and affiliate links. Once the initial effort has been made to create the magazine, ongoing maintenance of content may only be required occasionally so that your magazine continues to provide value to readers.

This option is excellent for people who want to share knowledge on a subject while gaining consistent cash flow. Plus, magazines allow you to reach global audiences and potential subscribers worldwide!

HOW TO MONETIZE A DIGITAL MAGAZINE

The readership for digital publications continues to expand and diversify. As a result, those in the know can make substantial money without actively doing anything.

But figuring out how to actually make money from a digital magazine could appear daunting. Knowing all of the possible revenue-generation strategies might be mind-boggling.

1. ADVERTISING

Ad revenue is the primary source of income for online publications. However, when it comes to commercials, you have a few distinct options.

Much like in print magazines, you may incorporate ads into full-page spreads. These have the potential to look fantastic, which will undoubtedly attract the target audience's attention.

Alternatively, you may incorporate leaderboards, advertisement banners, and other features. This is compatible with Google's AdSense program, which makes them perfect for passive income generation.

It's important to tailor ad sizes to the many screens your audience might be used to, as it relates to viewing the content. For example, ads and pop-ups on mobile devices will need to be smaller to avoid distraction. Ideally, those who read it on a giant computer screen have more room to maneuver.

The best thing is that more businesses will approach you to collaborate if you have a large readership. That way, you won't have to go looking for them yourself.

2. SPONSORED CONTENT

Sponsored content is one of the best ways to monetize a digital magazine. It's like advertising, except with just one other company involved. This individual purchaser will pay for a whole category of your material.

In such instance, it is typically presented as a guest essay in an online magazine. Sponsorships might be enticed through the provision of bundled benefits to potential backers. By doing so, they are prompted to buy more than one item, which is good for business.

3. AFFILIATE MARKETING

Affiliate marketing is a great way to make money in the background. Therefore allowing you to advertise associated goods and services by including links in your articles. As a result, you will earn a commission on all sales made due to the reader's clickthrough and subsequent purchase.

Commission rates and average sale prices vary widely by industry and product. A lot more money can be made if plenty of people read your digital publication.

You can locate affiliate companies to collaborate with in several different ways. First, you can connect with other people in the industry by joining affiliate networks, online forums, and social media.

4. SUBSCRIPTION PLANS

One other lucrative option is to turn your business into a subscription service. Your magazine will soar to new heights with the help of a dedicated readership who regularly contributes content.

A steady monthly income is much more reliable than one based on sponsorships or advertising arrangements. A larger marketing budget and more content options are possible with increased resources.

Building lasting ties with your audience is made possible through subscriptions.

You can offer them special bonuses, advanced access to releases, and more. This gives the impression to the reader that more is being offered for the price. It's essential for fostering long-term client loyalty.

5. MAILING LISTS

As a last online revenue stream, reader mailing lists offer a great opportunity to stay in touch with your audience while generating revenue. They allow you to promote and sell related merchandise. In addition, you can provide news and other information about your publication.

Promote your live events and sell tickets to them through your newsletter. Subscription and product discounts, as well as other types of item discounts, can be shared.

A larger audience may be accessible through mailing lists as well. Many subscribers join who have yet to engage with your material. This is a fantastic method of luring visitors to your digital magazine from various sources.

LEARN HOW TO MONETIZE A DIGITAL MAGAZINE FAST

It's easy and fun to publish your online magazines. With this step-by-step guide to reference, you can start monetizing and generating passive income fast. In addition, you may also incorporate various forms of advertising, sponsored content, and more.

Consider MagLoft if you want a cost-effective, straightforward means of digitizing your magazine. They provide excellent digital services to help your content stand out. More importantly, you can rely on their support staff for assistance at any point in time.

DIGITAL PUBLICATIONS

It's no secret that digital publications are taking off! With more and more people accessing content on their phones, tablets, and computers, it's essential to have your magazine available digitally. Not only does this allow you to reach a much wider audience, but it also provides an excellent opportunity to monetize your publication.

So if you want to make money from your magazine or even supplement your existing income stream, it's important to consider how you can turn digital publishing into another source of passive income.

Whether you're looking for ways to generate revenue from sales of your digital magazines, through advertising or sponsored content, or by subscription plans and mailing lists - there are countless options to explore.

PRINT PUBLICATIONS

Print publications are still the most popular way to consume content, which remains true even with the rise of digital media. While you may think that print magazines are no longer viable when monetizing your publication, this couldn't be further from the truth. Print magazines have a long history of success as a revenue stream and remain relevant today.

One of the best ways to make money from a print magazine is through advertising. You can offer advertisers space in your magazine for their advertisements and then receive payment. Depending on what works best for your audience, these payments can range from one-off fees or regular subscription plans. Many publishers also explore sponsored content options where companies pay for their content to be featured in the magazine.

In addition to advertising and sponsored content, one of the most popular ways to monetize print magazines is through subscription plans. By offering readers special discounts or incentives for subscribing, you can encourage them to keep coming back for more content month after month. Additionally, by providing subscribers exclusive access to content or products, you can foster loyalty and create a long-term source of revenue.

Finally, print magazines also offer great opportunities for exploring merchandise options such as t-shirts, mugs, and other memorabilia related to your publication. By selling these items alongside your regular magazine issues, you can generate additional income streams that don't rely on advertising or subscriptions.

CHAPTER VII

DIGITAL MARKETING

The term "digital marketing" refers to promoting and selling goods and services over the Internet via digital mediums such as search engines, social networking sites, and pay-per-click (PPC) advertising.

Digital marketing lets you locate people interested in your brand, have conversations with them, and convert them into buyers.

The most important forms of digital marketing are search engine marketing, content marketing, pay-per-click advertising, social media marketing, and email marketing.

It involves creating content to market a product or service that consumers can use and earn sales commissions. This type of income requires some upfront work, such as creating content, setting up an online store, or investing in advertising campaigns. However, once these tasks are completed, digital marketing can be relatively automated and generate consistent passive income streams with minimal upkeep.

For those who have a knack for writing, digital marketing can be a great way to monetize their skills. Creating content related to products and services you know about and leveraging various digital channels, such as social networks and PPC campaigns, can help drive leads and boost sales. In addition, learning how to optimize websites and track analytics is essential for getting the most out of your passive income strategies.

One important thing to remember when it comes to digital marketing is that it takes time—sometimes months or even years—to start seeing returns on investment. Therefore, staying motivated and committed to generating consistent cash flow through this method is important. Nevertheless, with patience and dedication, it is possible to build an impressive and profitable passive income portfolio through digital marketing.

By utilizing the right strategies and tools, digital marketing can be an excellent way to build a sustainable business. With the proper guidance and direction, you can easily create multiple streams of passive income from digital marketing and reap the rewards for years to come.

SOCIAL MEDIA MARKETING

Social media marketing promotes products and services through platforms such as Facebook, Instagram, Twitter, LinkedIn, and YouTube. Businesses can target potential customers through these channels based on their geo-location and interests.

Social media marketing involves creating content that resonates with users, engaging them in conversation, and providing helpful information to increase brand awareness. Additionally, companies can use social media to reach out to influencers who have an established following.

Social media is an excellent tool for generating passive income because it allows you to reach a large audience without constantly investing in advertising campaigns or paying for expensive, online courses. Additionally, many social networks offer free tools like analytics that make it easier to track how well your campaigns are performing and identify opportunities for improvement.

Although it may take some time to establish yourself as an influencer on social media, the passive income potential can be significant. For example, by leveraging your knowledge and creating valuable content, you can use social media to make money from affiliate programs, sponsored posts, or digital products like e-books and courses.

Social media marketing is a great way to generate passive income if used correctly. With consistent effort, strategic planning, and creativity, it is possible to build a thriving online business through targeted campaigns on platforms like Twitter and Instagram.

ONLINE BRANDING

Using online branding to earn passive income is a wonderful way to reach a broad audience and build trust with potential customers. By creating a solid presence on different platforms, businesses can create an impactful brand that becomes associated with the product or service they are selling.

Online branding involves creating content for blog posts, social media posts, YouTube videos, and other forms of digital marketing. It requires putting together carefully crafted visuals such as logos and banners to help your company stand out from the competition.

The key to successful online branding is consistency. You must maintain a professional image across all channels so that customers can recognize you whenever they contact your business. Additionally, staying active on various platforms is essential to keep up with the latest trends and ensure your message reaches potential customers.

Once you have developed a robust online presence, you can leverage it to create passive income streams. This can include using affiliate links, creating courses or e-books, or selling ad space on your website. Utilizing these strategies consistently over time can generate a steady stream of passive income to help fuel your business's growth.

CONTENT MARKETING

Content marketing is one of the most effective methods for generating passive income. This involves creating and curating content such as blog posts, articles, podcasts and videos that offer valuable advice or information about a particular topic.

Content marketing can promote products and services, educate potential customers about your business's offerings, or provide general information on a specific subject. It helps to establish yourself as an authority in your industry by providing helpful resources to interested readers.

Content marketing can create multiple passive income streams through advertising revenue from sponsored posts and affiliate programs. You can also generate money through digital products like e-books or online courses people can purchase directly from your website.

Content marketing is an effective way to generate passive income if you are willing to publish quality content consistently. By leveraging the power of digital platforms such as websites and social media, you can create a steady stream of passive income that will help support your business's growth.

ONLINE ADVERTISING

Online advertising is one of the most popular methods for generating passive income. This involves using digital platforms such as Google Ads, Facebook Ads, and Instagram Ads to promote products or services to potential customers.

By leveraging these platforms, businesses can create targeted campaigns tailored to their target audience. In addition, by creating relevant and engaging ads, you can generate a steady stream of passive income from clicks or purchases made on your ads.

If you want to succeed with online advertising, it is essential to do extensive research on your target audience in order to craft messages that will resonate with them. Staying up-to-date on the latest trends in digital marketing will help ensure your campaigns are optimized for maximum effectiveness.

Overall, online advertising can serve as a great way to generate passive income if you are willing to dedicate the time and resources necessary for success. By utilizing digital platforms, businesses can create targeted campaigns to reach potential customers while simultaneously gaining additional revenue streams.

CHAPTER VIII

SOCIAL MEDIA INFLUENCER

People widely recognized as authorities on a given subject are called "influencers" in social media. They maintain active and extensive social media communities of people who share their passion for the subject matter and pay close attention to their every word by frequently posting about it. Companies highly value social media influencers because of their ability to generate buzz around a product and inspire their audience to buy it.

The two main ways that social media influencers generate passive income are by creating sponsored content for companies and through affiliate links to products and services. Sponsored posts are usually paid in full either upfront or monthly. Affiliate marketing involves promoting a website creation service or other product type and receiving commission-based payments or discounts when someone purchases after clicking the link shared with the influencer's audience.

Social media influencers can diversify their income streams by offering webinars and e-books, teaching classes online, consulting services, and charging subscription fees for exclusive access to specific content. Furthermore, they can outsource their social media tasks to a virtual assistant or use automation tools to manage their networks and increase their online presence.

The amount of time needed to become an influencer varies, but it typically takes three months to build up a solid base of followers. It's important to remember that building an audience is not a one-time event—it requires consistent effort day after day. Ideally you'll want to lean towards obtaining at least 100,000 followers to maximize the ability to gain passive income from your following. With the right strategy, through this method alone, you can eventually build up enough passive income to live off of.

TYPES OF INFLUENCERS

There are a variety of ways to categorize influencers. Amongst the most popular are content types, influence and the number of followers. Additionally, influencers can be categorized by the specific field, in which they work. This means that even while specific influencers may fall into a lower category by one measure, they may appear higher in the influence stakes when seen through a different lens. Many celebrities, for instance, have a massive impact on society because of their status as influencers. However, without specialized knowledge in a limited field, both groups have less influence on their audience. On the other hand, Nano- and even micro-influencers can significantly impact their communities. Those customers could be precious to a company whose product is marketed to that market.

In conclusion, influencers are in a great position to generate passive income. With the right tools and strategies, social media influencers can monetize their following over time. However, it is essential to remember that establishing yourself as an influencer takes consistent effort and dedication. Many influencers bring unique value to companies through their specialized knowledge and expertise. By understanding how you can become an influencer, you'll be better prepared to choose the path best suited for you.

INSTAGRAM

Instagram is one of the most popular social media platforms, making it a great place to start if you want to become an influencer. To get started, you'll need to create content regularly and work diligently to grow your following. Once you have some traction, you can start monetizing your content with sponsored posts or affiliate links. Consider also creating digital products like e-books or courses your audience can purchase from any platform. With enough dedication and commitment, you'll be on your way to generating passive income through Instagram!

FACEBOOK

Facebook is another rewarding platform for influencers. It offers a range of monetization options, from sponsored posts to digital products like e-books and courses. As with all others, to get started, you'll need to consistently create content and build a dedicated following. You can also use Facebook's Ads Manager tool to target specific audiences while boosting your reach. Earning passive income through Facebook is rewarding and can be lucrative given the right amount of perseverance!

YOUTUBE

YouTube is one of the world's most popular social media platforms, making it an ideal place to start if you want to become an influencer. To get started, you'll need to create quality content that viewers will be interested in viewing. Once you have established yourself on the platform, you can begin monetizing your content with sponsored posts or affiliate links. Consider also creating digital products like e-books or courses that your audience can purchase from any platform. One of our former interns started a YouTube channel, which resulted in monthly five-figure earnings. So with exemplary dedication, strategy and a good measure of hard work, it's totally possible to generate passive income through YouTube!

TIKTOK

TikTok is one of the fastest-growing social media platforms and yet another great place to start if you want to become an influencer. First, you'll have to create content on a regular basis and work diligently to grow your. Once you start getting some traction, you can monetize your content with sponsored posts or affiliate links. But, also consider creating digital products such as e-books and courses your audience can purchase online. Because generating passive income through TikTok is one of the newest ways to earn cash without trading time for money.

These are just a few ways you can use social media platforms to generate passive income. Creating content regularly and building relationships with your followers are both crucial if you want to succeed. So if you're looking to create a steady income that will last for years, consider becoming a social media influencer.

CHAPTER VIIII

PODCASTING

The podcasting medium is here to stay. But do you ever consider starting one of your own?

In what capacity have you most recently engaged with podcasts? There's a good possibility that someone you know has listened lately, even if it's been a while since you did. There is a massive opening for podcast expansion thanks to the prevalence of mobile devices and the evolution of people's habits when it comes to consuming material.

There is also the matter of strategy. For example, podcasts have received significant investments from audio-focused tech companies like Spotify and Apple.

Deeper involvement is encouraged by podcasts because it's unusual to discover something that can keep your attention for 30 minutes or more. In addition, you can listen to a podcast while doing other things, like cooking or driving. Blog articles and other visual media have different limitations.

Several positive outcomes can result from launching a podcast, including exposure to new audiences, reduced levels of competition, and the opportunity to build rapport with your listeners. And the initial investment is much smaller than you might imagine. These are ideal things to know when starting a podcast that everyone will love.

With the right approach and investment in podcasting, you can earn passive income from your show. The key is to offer value-for-money sponsorships or sell merchandise associated with your brand's content. In addition, it's possible to extend your influence even further by repurposing recorded audio into other forms such as e-books, online courses, and books.

Podcasting is a great way to gain passive income. It allows people to record and share audio content with the world, providing listeners with hours of entertainment. With podcasting, you can create multiple passive income streams through advertisements, sponsorships, affiliate marketing, and more.

It's about more than just the money, though, because podcasts give you a platform to share your story and pass on knowledge while being heard by thousands worldwide - something that would only be possible with modern technology. So if you're willing to invest in podcasting, plenty of rewards are waiting for you!

The Steps of starting a podcast:

Launching a podcast may seem like an overwhelming task for those just beginning. However, with the helpful tips and resources I have provided below, you can get your podcast up and running in no time! To ensure the success of your new venture, take one week to arrange all items on this checklist before officially launching your show.

Here are the steps for starting a podcast:

1. Pick a topic: It's best to start with a general topic you are passionate about and have some working knowledge of.

2. Name your Podcast: Choose something unique, catchy, and memorable for your listeners.

3. Gather Equipment: You will need podcasting equipment such as microphones, audio editing software, a hosting/streaming service, and other accessories to record and produce quality sound episodes.

4. Create an Intro & Outro Sequence: This is how you will introduce yourself to your audience when they listen to each episode - think of it like an elevator pitch for the show!

5. Record Your Episodes: Keep in mind that creating podcasts is all about quality content, so make sure your episodes are engaging, informative, and entertaining.

6. Edit Your Audio: Use audio editing software to ensure every episode is professional sounding and ready for streaming.

7. Upload & Publish Episodes: Decide where you will publish your podcasts on iTunes, Spotify, or Google Play Music. You can also promote it via social media channels like Twitter or Instagram.

8. Promote Your Podcast: Make sure people know about your podcast by leveraging the power of marketing and advertising - create a website for your show, build an email list, create social media accounts, and much more.

9. Track Performance: Keep track of how well each episode is doing regarding views and downloads so that you can make adjustments as needed.

By following these nine steps, you'll be well on your way to launching a successful podcast and generating passive income from it.

Once you have established your show and built an audience, there are many ways to earn passive income. Some of the most popular methods include, offering sponsorships, selling merchandise, affiliate marketing, advertising, or even creating courses related to the topics discussed in each episode. All of which can help you build long-term residual income and provide a stable source of monthly cash flow.

THE COST OF STARTING A PODCAST

The cost of starting a podcast depends on your equipment, the hosting service you choose, and any other services you may need to make your show successful. Equipment such as microphones, stands and shock mounts can range from $50-$500, depending on what features you need. Hosting services for podcasts vary in price but generally start at around $10 per month. Any additional costs, such as music licensing or professional editing, will depend on the type of podcast you are creating and how much production value you want to add to each episode.

The average initial investment for starting a podcast can vary widely depending on the type of show you're creating and the production value you wish to incorporate. However, when starting out, most people invest an average of $100-$200 in equipment, hosting services, and other necessities. Depending on your individual goals and needs, this price range can go up or down. Ultimately, the cost of starting a podcast will depend on your vision for the show, the level of production quality you're striving for, and the amount of time you have to learn the necessary skills to make it all happen.

CHAPTER X

BLOGGING

There is a good reason why 600 million blogs are currently being updated worldwide. Blogging is rewarding in many ways, whether for fun or for a living.

Establishing a blog is an effective promotional tool for businesses. It improves your search engine rankings and helps you connect with your target audience, among other benefits.

All bloggers, amateurs, or paid journalists, can benefit from using a blog. It's a great way to share your ideas with the world and learn more about the things that interest you. In addition, it's an excellent resource for building credibility as an expert in your field, growing your brand, and even monetizing your online presence.

Whatever your motivation for starting a blog may be, it's become an essential tool for expanding your reach and establishing authority in the digital sphere.

Beginners guide to help you get started.

Starting a blog doesn't have to be daunting. On the contrary, it can be surprisingly simple! Here are some essential tips for getting started:

CHOOSE A BLOG NICHE

As a new blogger, it would be best if you zeroed in on a specific topic or niche to gain readers. But how do you choose where to direct your attention?

Consider your ultimate objectives first. Is it the intent to spread the word about your company? Disseminate knowledge or indulge in a hobby? Monetize your writing? Ideally, thinking about why you're starting a blog in the first place can help you find the best niche. Whether you want to share insights about your profession, explore your passions in-depth, or make money off your efforts.

Your blog's focus will be the defining characteristic of your online persona, so carefully consider it. Zero in on something you are enthusiastic about and possess a wealth of knowledge in.

You may narrow your target demographic even further depending on your level of expertise. For example, you could specialize in low-cost European vacations or vegan cooking, sub-genres within the more extensive travel and food industries.

RESEARCH YOUR AUDIENCE

Undoubtedly one of the most common blunders made by new bloggers? Falsely assuming that everyone in the room shares your views. Knowing your intended audience is just as important, as knowing what you'll write about. Think about the people you anticipate reading your blog and how their interests align with the content you plan to post. For example, are you targeting the business elite? Is it the yoga community? Women who are expecting?

The idea it to list what they're into, what hurts, and what they need. Then, determine what they might be interested in learning about or what problems they might face based on your knowledge of their personalities.

Incorporate these thoughts into your blog's topic selection and writing processes. It's important to know why the content you're writing will be helpful to your readers before you start writing it.

DRAW INSPIRATION ONLINE

Starting in the blogging world, you may wonder where to find inspiration for posts. Naturally, brainstorming is a fantastic tactic. But it also helps to research. That way you can figure out which topics are in demand.

Examine alternative business blogs as a starting point. First, keep an eye out for the subjects they discuss. Then, using a tool like BuzzSumo for competitor analysis, you can see which of your rivals' articles generate the most interest (in the form of clicks or social media shares).

LEARN WHAT PEOPLE ARE SEARCHING FOR

Research relevant keywords as you compile your list of topics. This method involves tailoring your article's content to specific keywords and phrases your intended readers will use to find your work in online search engines.

You don't have to be a keyword research expert, but it helps to know what people are looking for. If you want your content to be read, you need to ensure it shows up in search engine results, which will help you do that.

USE KEYWORDS STRATEGICALLY

Doing keyword research to learn what your readers are interested in will help you write more effectively, but you should also use those keywords naturally throughout the text. For starters, include relevant keywords in the article's title and body. This aids Google in comprehending the nature of your content.

STRUCTURE YOUR BLOG BY CATEGORY

You should categorize your blog posts. When you first launch your blog, organize the content so that it's simple for visitors to find the information they seek. For instance, the site's menu might benefit from overarching topic subheadings.

Google likes this structure, too; it's a factor in determining which articles get prioritized in search results. Therefore, maintaining well-defined blog categories is a win-win.

KEEP YOUR CONTENT UP-TO-DATE

A second essential piece of advice for new bloggers is to update regularly. As a first step, focus on creating evergreen content, such as blog posts that cover a topic, which will always be of interest to readers. Yet, even with the most evergreen articles, you should regularly update your posts to maintain interest.

It's possible to do anything from a quick refresher to a complete overhaul when updating. By looking at how well a post does, you can estimate how often it will need to be updated (more on that later).

Include a column in your editorial calendar reminding you to revisit the article 6 months after it has been published to check for updates.

CREATE A BLOG NEWSLETTER

There will still be a lingering question after you've written a month's worth of articles and published them. When promoting your blog, how do you plan on drawing in readers?

It would be best if you first thought about ways to interest visitors who have already found your website. A successful website relies on repeat visitors who aren't just casual browsers but loyal followers.

You can publish a regular email newsletter and solicit subscriptions from your blog entries. Include a call to action within your content that prompts readers to subscribe so you can begin amassing email addresses. This will allow you to have constant, one-on-one contact with your audience, which is crucial for converting casual browsers into devoted supporters.

Innovative strategies for collecting email addresses from your readers should be explored. One strategy is to ask for their contact information in exchange for a downloadable freebie, such as a webinar, e-book, guide, or template.

PROMOTE YOUR BLOG ON SOCIAL MEDIA

The next challenge is attracting fresh eyes, readers who have never seen your blog before.

Publicizing your blog posts on social media is a quick, easy, and cost-effective strategy. When promoting your blog on social media, ensure it has its own profile and uses your logo as the profile picture. Then, post and promote all of your blog entries on your social media platforms. If you want people to click your link, you have to use a compelling image, title, and caption.

Aside from disseminating the articles yourself, you can also rally your network to do the same. Put share buttons for various social media platforms prominently on your page to encourage readers to spread the word. A simple request for readers to share your post can be left at the end.

BUYING A BLOG

If you want to accelerate the process, consider buying an already-established blog. This can be a great way to jumpstart your website and gain access to well-written content with existing links and followers. When buying a blog, look into its status, ranking, statistics, and reputation to make an informed decision. If a blog has been around for some time, it's less likely that its content will need updating or editing before publication. The flip side is that such blogs are more expensive than those just starting.

When buying a blog, get access to the backend analytics to track performance and measure ROI. In addition, be sure to use a secure payment method for transferring funds and confirm that you have rights to the content in writing. Finally, it's important to research industry standards when setting up contracts with buyers or sellers. This will help ensure you get the best deal and protect you from potential legal issues. Taking these precautions may not seem necessary at first glance, but they are critical to ensure you don't get burned. Buying an established blog is a great way to jumpstart your passive income venture.

STARTING A BLOG

Starting a blog from scratch may be the best option if you plan on writing your own content. To do this, you need to have some basic technical know-how or be willing to hire someone who does.

The first thing to consider is what platform you want to use for your blog. Popular options include WordPress and Blogger. Both are user-friendly platforms with plenty of features that can quickly get you started with blogging. Spend time researching both options and determining which is most suitable for your needs.

When setting up your blog, think about how you want it to look and function aesthetically. Be sure to include relevant information such as contact details, an easy-to-navigate menu, and critical pages like an "About" page.

Once your blog is ready, start writing! Aim to post regularly. This will help keep your content fresh and attract more readers. As you become exceedingly experienced in blogging, explore different promotion methods, such as guest posting on other sites, joining online communities related to your topic, or being paid to advertise (if budget allows).

Lastly, don't forget to monetize your blog – the ultimate goal is to gain passive income. Consider ways such as displaying ads on your site, offering affiliate links for products you recommend, or even selling digital products like e-books and webinars.

CHAPTER XI

MUSIC DISTRIBUTION

Music distribution is the key to success for every musician who wants to reach their target audience upon the release of their music. To reach your potential audience, you must engage in music distribution, which means sending your finished song to music providers such as major streaming sites, radio stations, advertising agencies, etc.

Distributing your music is the first step in getting it heard by those who will fall in love with it. If you're immersed in the music business, you might be wondering where to start with putting your music online for digital distribution amongst the fan base, which happens to be crucial.

Music distribution is a great way to generate passive income. You can become an independent artist and upload your music to third-party platforms such as Spotify, iTunes, or Amazon Music. These sites pay royalties each time your songs are streamed or purchased, giving you a steady income after your music's initial setup and marketing. Additionally, you will receive a percentage of live performances wherever you play your music. This option requires some upfront costs for equipment and production but can be very lucrative in the long run with proper management and promotion. Keep in mind, with streaming services growing in popularity, getting your songs out there and earning money can be challenging!

LICENSING YOUR MUSIC

This involves selling the right to use your composition by other people in their projects, like TV shows, advertisements, and video games. It's typically done through third-party companies that license music for various uses and pay royalties for every play of the song or use of the audio file. With more and more media outlets looking for original content, licensing your music could be highly profitable if you can produce quality tracks that fit specific requirements.

In addition, if you own the copyright on any of your songs (meaning you wrote it, composed it, and produced it), then all money generated from plays falls back into your pocket with no need to share profits. Thus, music licensing can be a great way to generate passive income.

While it does require more upfront work than streaming services, once your songs have been licensed and placed in various projects, you will earn money for them repeatedly with no further effort. This can be an excellent way to generate residual income if you can reach the right people or companies that need quality audio content.

PUBLISHING ROYALTIES

Publishing royalties are payments to you for songwriters or composers when their songs are performed publicly, sold through digital downloads, streamed online, broadcast on TV or radio, and other sources. The amount of money writers get from publishing royalties depends on various factors, such as the song's popularity, how often it is played, and what media outlet it is featured on (e.g., radio station vs. streaming service).

The great thing about publishing royalties is that they generate a steady income stream with minimal effort after signing up with a publishing company. Depending on your agreement with the publisher and the outlets in which your music is featured, you could make hundreds or even thousands of dollars each month passively from this income.

MONETIZATION

Monetization is the process of turning your creative content into a profitable asset. For example, this can be done by displaying ads on your music videos or website, selling merchandise (e.g., t-shirts, mugs) related to your music, and offering exclusive fan packages. The great thing about monetizing your content is that once you have established an audience, you can continue to make money from it for years without putting in any extra effort.

By establishing multiple streams of passive income from these sources, you can make money from your passion and creativity without wasting too much time or energy. Each method has its setup process and potential earnings, so it's important to research and figure out which will work best for you and your goals.

With the right strategy, you can make passive income from music and enjoy a comfortable lifestyle without worrying about money! This guide has outlined some of the most popular ways independent artists and musicians generate passive income – start exploring them today and see which works best for you.

CHAPTER XII

DOMAIN FLIPPING

The overarching tactic underlying domain switching is straightforward. Domain names are the distinctive addresses for websites, and they must be registered before they may be used by anyone else.

You can get the domain name outright if it is still for sale. However, if someone else is already using the domain name, you'll need to make an offer to buy it from them.

Buying a domain name at a low price and then selling it for a profit is called "domain flipping." The next step is to sell the domain to an interested party for a profit rather than using it yourself.

To succeed at domain flipping, you must research and understand the domain name market. First, you should track which domains are in demand and their historical prices. In addition, you should find out what keywords have the highest search engine rankings for those domains. Doing homework can help determine when a domain is worth buying or selling.

WHY WOULD YOU FLIP A DOMAIN?

Justify your actions. Financial gain is the primary motivator. Domains are akin to prime real estate on the Internet and can reap a profit. Many investors specialize in buying and selling domain names as part of their income strategy.

But flipping an existing domain for a higher price isn't the only option available; you may also consider developing the domain into something else, such as a blog or website, to increase its value. This could involve coding the site or adding content, depending on what the domain is about.

STEPS FOR FLIPPING A DOMAIN

Let's say you want to consider selling a domain name. Where do you start? What must you do?

1. SEARCH FOR A DOMAIN

Finding a domain name worthy of purchase is the first step. Next, find a domain that is cheap to buy yet could yield a high profit if you want to maximize your return on investment (ROI).

First-time domains can be found using any number of resources; for instance, you could conduct a name search to look for available domains relevant to a particular service, product, or subject area.

Another option is to visit a domain auction, where you can see a long list of domains that are currently for sale. Finally, if you're looking for alternatives, remember to peruse the auctions for lapsed domain names.

2. EVALUATE THE DOMAIN

When a domain name fits your investment budget, you should consider it carefully. A domain name's prospective worth is based on various criteria, including:

- Length
- Brandability

- Relevance
- Search friendliness

If you want to know whether the domain will be worth more to you in the long run than what you paid, you should do some digging. Look at similar recently sold domains and their price histories.

3. REGISTER THE DOMAIN NAME

You may buy the domain and have it registered in your name if everything checks out. This is typically a quick and easy process.

4. FIND A BUYER FOR THE DOMAIN

This is the most challenging part and has the most room for error.

You can profit from a domain flip if you locate a buyer prepared to pay more than you paid.

There are several ways to approach this; one option is to "purchase and hold" or do as little as possible while waiting for the domain's value to rise.

If you want to sell your domain, interested parties can locate your contact information in the registry you make public. They might also make a private offer or place a bid.

Alternatively, you could take a more proactive approach by creating a landing page for your domain to attract potential buyers. If you want to move quickly, you can put your domain up for auction.

5. SELL THE DOMAIN

In the end, your buyer will pay you for the domain and take possession once they've registered a new name under the name server. This is another straightforward process that only requires a little bit of time.

THE BEST PLACE FOR DOMAIN FLIPPING

Domain flipping consists of two primary actions: purchasing and reselling. If you choose a comprehensive domain marketplace like GoDaddy, you can do both in one location.

If you have specific requirements or would like to implement a systematic approach, a specialized tool may interest you.

The domain drop-catching technique, for instance, necessitates the use of a tool that can locate recently expired or soon-to-be-expired domains. Domains like ExpiredDomains.net and JustDropped.com are frequently used. In addition, GoDaddy Auctions' is a great outlet for purchasing expired domain names and has proven successful.

If you're looking to attract private sellers, you should not use an auction or marketplace once you've secured the domain name.

While auctions can speed things up, some names are better off being kept on the market for a long period of time. Everything will be determined by the nature of the domain you're selling and the probable buyer pool.

HOW MUCH MONEY SHOULD YOU SET ASIDE MONTHLY TO INVEST IN DOMAIN NAMES?

What sort of initial investment is required to make a profit from trading domain names? In all honesty, I can't say. Domains can be purchased for as little as a few dollars and as much as hundreds of millions of dollars, and it is possible, to begin with just one domain to flip. So if you have $10, you can go into domain flipping.

But domain flipping can be a game of chance.

Some domains can take months, or even years, to sell. It's also possible that you will only make money off some of your cheap domains, but selling just one for $1,000 might turn your business around.

If you want to make money trading domain names, you should stockpile a wide variety of them. In light of this, a budget of a few hundred dollars is recommended.

When is the best time to flip a domain to make the most cash?

Domain flipping is often unpredictable. Your domain flipping technique will be more successful if you buy a domain before most people recognize its value or sell it at its peak popularity.

So when is the "best" time to flip a domain? While there are many variables to consider, the most significant moment to purchase a domain is when it receives little attention. This could mean taking advantage of a domain's infancy, when a new product or concept is still relatively unknown, or when the domain's original register has expired.

Domain sales have a considerably more nuanced timeline.

After finishing your registration, auctioning off your items may be the ideal alternative if you need quick cash. Although some domains benefit from only a few incubation periods before being flipped, others may require months or even years of holding time. The optimal time to sell depends on the type of domain you have.

WHAT KINDS OF DOMAINS ARE BEST FOR FLIPPING?

Which domain names are best for reselling? It's tough to say, but you'll have better luck looking for low-cost domains that can yield a high sale price.

The following characteristics can be found in good domain names to flip:

EXPIRED

Registry-expired domain names typically go for less than their functional equivalents. But, again, this is because they are making a comeback after being absent, and the owner could be more concerned with making a profit.

There is no need to outbid other domain investors at a public auction or to offer a large private bid to entice a private holder. In reality, you're just seizing a new, cheap chance.

SHORT

Domain investors should proceed with caution when purchasing short domain names. It's safe to assume that the shorter a domain name is, the more money you can expect to make. This is because shorter domain names are more convenient for users in terms of typing, remembering, and promoting. In general, you should expect a more significant return on investment if you can purchase a short domain name (three to five letters) or one that contains a common phrase.

The problem is that most other domain-hunters are aware of this principle and are actively hunting for short domains alongside you. As a result, the costs are driven up, which means you might not be able to include them as a central part of your plan if your funds are limited.

NEW

Also of great value are brand-new domains. There are opportunities to make money when new domain name extensions and variations appear, and you can jump on these trends before anybody else can.

You may get a leg up on the competition and reap the benefits of new products, services, and ideas by snatching up a domain at the start of its development. For instance, Cryptocurrency is a relatively recent idea; had you recognized its potential and acted swiftly, you could have purchased a domain name like Cryptocurrency.com for pennies on the dollar. Imagine what it's worth now!

LOCAL

You can actually make lots of money by flipping a locally focused domain name.

They're niche enough that you won't have to compete with many other sellers but high quality enough that they'll generate a decent profit when you do. For example, if the domain name you want, HotDogs.com, is already taken, you might have better luck with YourCityHereHotDogs.com, which contains your city's name in the URL.

KEYWORD-FRIENDLY

It's also important to consider how well optimized the domain name is for search engines (SEO). For example, Google's Keyword Planner allows you to research a given topic to discover which keywords and phrases are most frequently used in connection with that specific topic.

A keyword or phrase frequently searched for will increase the value of a domain name. As with short domain names, the challenge is that more rivals may pursue these promising openings.

If you're interested in making money through exploring the world of online real estate, flipping domain names is a possible option. Of course, to be successful, you'll need some knowledge, a keen eye, and good timing, but if you stick with it, you can build a sustainable income.

CHAPTER XIII

STOCK PHOTOS

The word "stock photography" refers to any generic image that anybody can use for any purpose, including but not limited to news articles, blogs, websites, advertisements, and promotional materials.

With stock photos, you can upload your images to sites like Shutterstock or Adobe Stock and get paid every time someone downloads them. You can even set up a subscription service with some websites so that your customers pay monthly for access to your pictures. Additionally, there are many other websites where you can sell stock photos, such as Fotolia, Bigstock, Dreamstime, 123RF, and iStockPhoto.

You can create stock photos by taking high-quality photographs that people would be interested in using for their purposes. This could include anything from landscapes and portraits to product shots or concept art. It's important to remember that you should never take photos of people without their permission, and any images featuring identifiable landmarks, like the Eiffel Tower, must be credited to the original creator.

When your images are ready for upload, most websites have a simple drag-and-drop feature to quickly add them to the platform. Each website requires different information when uploading pictures, such as keywords and captions, so make sure you read up on each one's guidelines before submitting anything. Once everything is uploaded correctly, it can take anywhere from a few days to several weeks for your images to get approved.

Once your stock photos are live, sales will often come in slowly at first but steadily increase over time with more active marketing or if the image becomes popular in search results. In addition, some websites offer bonuses and discounts for photographers who reach certain sales milestones or consistently upload quality content.

Stock photography is an easy way to generate passive income, as it requires minimal effort once you learn the basics of taking good pictures and uploading them correctly. It's an excellent opportunity for anyone looking to make money on the side without having to put in too much work. Plus, it's a fun way to explore your creativity and potentially turn your passion into something that earns you money!

By following these steps, you can make passive income with stock photos in no time.

CHALLENGES OF BEING A STOCK PHOTOGRAPHER

It's sad, but most people give up after the first six months. The main reason is perhaps they desired to make more money within the first few months. However, there are other factors involved.

It's usually because of low quality images, although this is only sometimes the case. Furthermore, there is the issue of competing with thousands of other contributors for 15 years' worth of shares. Quite honestly, it requires a lot of time and effort to post 100 photographs per month and carefully label them all.

It takes ingenuity to stand out in a crowded industry, let alone one where content creation is already difficult. It's more complex than it sounds to make commercial material (something that someone would want to buy right now, ideally a business) and copyright it correctly.

Finally, the legal aspect of stock photography can be tricky to navigate and often needs clarification for newcomers. Staying up-to-date on any changes in the law or regulations will ensure you stay legally compliant when offering your services as a stock photographer.

CHAPTER XIIII

DROPSHIPPING

In dropshipping, the retailer does not retain any of the items the customer orders in stock. Instead, to meet customer demand, the seller makes periodic stock purchases from an outside source (often a wholesaler or manufacturer).

Unlike traditional retail, dropshipping's most notable distinction is that the selling merchant does not stock or own inventory; instead, they serve as a middleman between the customer and supplier.

When a customer orders, the seller will place the same order with their dropshipping partner or list of suppliers. The drop shipper then fulfills the order on behalf of the retailer, usually shipping directly to the customer's doorstep.

Dropshipping is an attractive business model for many because it requires little to no capital expenditure and can therefore be started relatively quickly with minimal upfront costs. It also allows sellers to focus on marketing and sales instead of fulfillment and offer a wider variety of products without investing in additional inventory. In addition, selling through dropshipping often results in faster delivery times and more reliable services than those offered by traditional retailers.

Instead of storing and transporting things directly, "drop shippers" purchase inventory and fulfillment logistics from a third party. Because dropshipping relies on a third-party provider for inventory warehousing and order fulfillment, a single person or a large team can run a dropshipping firm.

HOW DOES DROPSHIPPING WORK

For drop shipping to work, there must be a connection between the storefront and the manufacturer.

When deciding to implement a dropshipping strategy, two primary options typically arise. The first is to independently use a supplier database to find one or more wholesale vendors. AliExpress, SaleHoo, and Worldwide Brands are some of the most well-known online supplier databases.

If you want to avoid spending time locating suppliers for each product you want to sell, you can use an app that puts you in touch with thousands of vendors.

Most of the dropshipping work is now automated. As the shop owner, all you need to do is double-check the information and place the order. Then, no matter where they are in the world, the buyer receives the merchandise directly from the AliExpress vendor.

It's common to think of dropshipping as a simple way to make money quickly. Nonetheless, that's not the case. Your startup e-commerce site requires the same level of commitment as any other online store. A growing eCommerce firm can benefit from partnering with a dependable and convenient dropshipping company to speed up order and fulfillment processes.

BENEFITS OF DROPSHIPPING

Dropshipping has several advantages as an eCommerce strategy, and this outline will highlight several.

1. LESS UPFRONT CAPITAL REQUIRED

The most significant benefit of dropshipping is opening an online shop with a minimal initial investment in stock. On the contrary, traditionally, an enormous portion of a store's or online shop's capital is ordinarily invested in the stock.

In the dropshipping business model, you don't invest in inventory until after you've made a sale and collected payment from the buyer. Dropshipping allows you to get started with minimal expenditure because you don't need to start with a large inventory.

Launching a dropshipping store is safer than other online shops because you don't have to worry about selling all the stock you buy at once.

2. EASY TO START

Running an online store is a breeze when you don't have to maneuver actual goods. For example, drop shipping eliminates the need for you to handle the following:

- Controlling or bearing the costs of a storage facility
- Shipping out your purchases
- Accounting which requires a system for keeping tabs on the stock
- Dealing with incoming shipments and returns
- Keeping up with constant product orders and inventory management

3. LOW OVERHEAD

You save on administrative costs because you don't have to worry about stocking shelves or supervising warehouses. Numerous thriving online dropshipping shops are operated out of the owner's home with not much more than a laptop computer and some regular overhead.

These expenses will rise as your business expands, but they will remain significantly lower than a storefront of a similar size.

4. FLEXIBLE LOCATION

In today's world, all you need to run a profitable business is access to the Internet and a dropshipping strategy. However, the success of every company hinges on its management team's ability to maintain open lines of communication with its suppliers and promptly deliver services and support to customers that consistently exceed their expectations.

5. WIDE SELECTION OF PRODUCTS TO SELL

As a result of not having to stock your shelves in advance, you can provide consumers with a wide selection of the latest and greatest products. Additionally, you can switch up your dropshipping product list without worrying about the unsold stock. A product can be added to your online shop at no extra charge if your supplier has it in stock.

6. EASIER TO TEST

Dropshipping is a viable fulfillment option if you're opening a new store or want to gauge client interest in related or unrelated categories (such as accessories or new product lines). But, again, the critical advantage of dropshipping is that you may list and sell things before investing heavily in inventory.

7. EASIER TO SCALE

If you run a standard retail operation and suddenly get three times as many orders as normal, you'll have to put in three times as many hours. However, if you use dropshipping providers, they'll handle much of the extra work that comes with fulfilling your customers' orders as you develop.

Brands that use dropshipping scales better than regular eCommerce businesses, even though more sales always necessitate more work, especially in customer care.

DRAWBACKS OF DROPSHIPPING

With all the advantages we've discussed, dropshipping is an excellent option for any business wishing to launch an online store or increase its product selection. However, dropshipping has drawbacks, just as with any other method. In most cases, you may pay more for ease and adaptability.

Before jumping into a dropshipping business, consider these drawbacks.

1. LOW-PROFIT MARGINS

Competitive dropshipping markets have low-profit margins. Competition for customers is fierce in the dropshipping industry since new stores can spring up overnight and operate with almost no overhead expenditures. As a result, they can get by on razor-thin profit margins because they put so little into getting the company off the ground.

You may set yourself apart from other dropshippers in the industry by avoiding suppliers with subpar websites and non-existent or inadequate customer support. However, shoppers will still check your prices against your competitors.

A rise in a rivalry like this soon eats away at any profit margins that might have existed in a particular market.

2. INVENTORY ISSUES

Inventory management becomes a breeze if you have all your products in stock. However, stock levels can frequently fluctuate when you source from numerous warehouses that also process orders for other retailers.

Thankfully, a few tools available nowadays allow you to synchronize with vendors. For example, drop shippers can "pass along" customer orders to a dropshipping supplier with as few as two clicks, and the supplier's stock level should be visible in real-time.

3. SHIPPING COMPLEXITIES

Most dropshippers work with many suppliers, meaning that your online store's products could come from several distinct dropshippers. This effectively removes your ability to influence the production process.

Scenario: a customer needs to buy three different products, and they can get them exclusively from three different vendors. It would be unwise to pass on the three shipping costs you'll incur for sending each item to the consumer. However, automating these dropshipping calculations can be challenging, even when it makes it logical to include them.

4. SUPPLIER ERRORS

Do you recall when you had to take the blame for something that wasn't your fault?

The most reliable dropshippers still make mistakes from time to time while sending out orders, and if this occurs, you should be the one to take the blame and provide an apology. It would be in your best interest to work with dependable suppliers known to deliver high-level customer satisfaction. Because inadvertently, unreliable or poor-quality suppliers could hurt your company's reputation by delivering damaged products or providing poor customer service.

5. LIMITED CUSTOMIZATION AND BRANDING

Dropshipping removes the need for custom manufacturing or print-on-demand, limiting your ability to influence the final product. In most cases, the supplier also creates the product's packaging and brand.

Depending on the dropshipper, product modifications may be possible. However, even in that case, the product itself is still largely under the supplier's sway. A manufacturer would often request a minimum order quantity before making any modifications or additions to a product.

CHAPTER XV

PRINT ON DEMAND

Print-on-demand (or POD) is a revolutionary order fulfillment technique where items are printed right when an order is made - and Printful's version doesn't require any minimum orders. With POD, you can design unique products that reflect your brand identity, offering them to customers as distinctive merchandise.

Print-on-demand is an easy and cost-effective way for entrepreneurs to launch new products without investing in large quantities of inventory. Print-on-demand businesses allow you to design products like t-shirts, mugs, pins, and other items that can be printed with your designs and sold online. This business requires a minimal upfront investment, as the printing company handles all production and fulfillment services.

All you have to do is create a design, upload it to their platform, and they take care of the rest. Print-on-demand services allow you to start generating passive income immediately without purchasing, storing, or shipping any physical products.

PRINT-ON-DEMAND PROS AND CONS

Print-on-demand is a great way to start an online store without significant capital investments. Still, it's important to understand the pros and cons associated with this business model.

Pros:

- No upfront investment is required

- Low risk because you don't have to purchase inventory in bulk

- Easy setup and quick turnaround

- Little effort needed - the printing company handles all production and fulfillment services

Cons:

- Limited product selection

- Lower profit margins than other business models

- You can only control the quality of your products if you produce them yourself

Whether print-on-demand is the right choice for you, depends on your unique situation. But it's certainly an option worth considering if you want to start generating passive income without a significant investment of time or money. The print-on-demand method allows you to easily create unique products and sell them online with minimal effort.

Print-on-demand is an excellent way to quickly launch an online store without taking on substantial risks or investing heavily in inventory. Of course, whether it's the right choice will depend solely on your individual needs and goals, but this business model can serves as a good way to generate passive income.

T-SHIRTS

This happens to be one of my personal favorites. I once sold 200 shirts of the same style earning $19,800 over time. Although selling t-shirts isn't my primary source of income, it's definitely one of the 25 passive income strategies I find most reliable, and for years to come.

Designing and selling t-shirts is one of the most popular methods for generating passive income. Using print-on-demand services like Printful, you can start a t-shirt business without investing in inventory. All you need to do is create your design, upload it to the platform, and they take care of the rest – from printing to fulfillment and shipping. It's that easy!

The great thing about t-shirts is that you can create them for any occasion or event. So, people will be willing to buy all kinds of designs, from funny slogans to sports teams or political statements. Plus, with no upfront investment needed, this is an easy way to test different designs and determine the most successful ones.

HOODIES

In addition to t-shirts, you can also use print-on-demand services to create other apparel such as hoodies, tank tops, sweatshirts, and more. As with t-shirts, you can design these items for any occasion or event. Whether it's a funny saying or an image that someone might relate to – there are all kinds of possibilities when creating unique designs.

BACKPACKS AND BAGS

If apparel isn't your thing, you can create bags and backpacks with print-on-demand services. These are great for travelers, students and professionals – anyone who needs a bag to carry their items.

You can design bags with unique patterns or prints that reflect your brand identity. For example, you could create a basic design in various colors to give customers more choices. With no upfront investment needed, this is another easy way to generate passive income, without the risks.

HATS

Hats are another great product to offer through print-on-demand services. Create custom designs that reflect your brand and reach out to potential customers interested in purchasing them.

MUGS AND DRINKWARE

Print-on-demand services are also a great way to create mugs and drinkware. People love personalized mugs for special occasions, for friends, family members, or just for themselves. You could design these items with funny sayings or images that people can relate to or even offer them in different colors and designs.

Overall, there are endless possibilities for generating passive income using print-on-demand services. From apparel to bags and hats, you can easily create unique products that reflect your brand identity while reaching out to potential customers interested in purchasing them. Considering there's no upfront investment, this is an easy way to start building a passive income stream with very little effort.

HOW MUCH DOES PRINTFUL SUBSCRIPTIONS COST?

Printful offers a range of subscription plans and pricing structures, so you can find the one that best suits your needs. The company's basic plan is free, with no setup fees or monthly costs. For more features and flexibility, several paid plans are available starting from $14 per month (plus extra costs for products).

The paid plans include access to a wider range of products and materials (including apparel, bags, mugs, drinkware, hats, and more), automated order fulfillment services, and priority customer support.

Depending on the level of service desired, you can choose the right plan that suits your budget. With Printful's subscription plans, you can quickly generate passive income without any upfront costs or risks.

Printful Pro subscription plans offer a range of features and services designed for businesses looking to generate passive income through their print-on-demand service. Their monthly plan is $49/per month, and the yearly plan is $593/per year.

The Pro subscription provides an extensive range of products and materials, including t-shirts, hoodies, bags, backpacks, hats, and mugs. And with automated order fulfillment services included in the plan, it's that much easier to start generating passive income right away!

You also get priority customer support with the Pro plan, so if you ever have any questions or issues, you can get help almost instantly. Plus, there are no setup fees or hidden costs. All you need to do is pay your subscription fee each month (or annually) to continue using their services.

Printful Pro subscription plans are perfect for anyone looking to gain consistent cash flow. With no upfront investment needed and automated order fulfillment services included in the plan – it's easy to see why this is a fantastic way to create yet another passive income stream with very little effort.

CHAPTER XVI

VENDING MACHINES

Very few vending machines make more than $5 every week. However, a strategically located vending machine can generate significantly more than that, often exceeding $100 per week and reaching into the hundreds of dollars per day range. Several factors affect how much money vending machines make.

The vending machine industry is unique among businesses. Earnings from vending machines are considered passive income because they do not require the owner's constant attention. On the other hand, family-owned diners typically provide owners with active income because the owner acts as the business's manager and head chef.

Starting a vending machine business requires careful financial planning and preparation. Create an enterprise plan that addresses all of the following:

- Location of the vending machines
- Costs associated with purchasing and operating the machines
- Maintenance and repair issues
- The type of merchandise to be sold
- Marketing a product or service.

While vending machines may seem easy to make money on the side, every successful business involves careful financial planning and budgeting. Planning for your business should include registering it with the state and acquiring the necessary vending permissions, which differ from state to state and even from city to city. Visit your local secretary of state's website to learn more about incorporating your business and to determine what licenses are required.

WHERE CAN VENDING MACHINES BE PURCHASED?

Vending machines can be purchased online or in person. Popular online stores, including Amazon and eBay, have a variety of vending machines available for purchase. Used vending machine auctions are held regularly by established companies such as Vending Solutions and ReCarbon.

When shopping for a vending machine, remember to consider factors such as the size of the machine, its price range, and what kind of merchandise it will dispense. For instance, if you want to sell candy bars or soft drinks from your vending machine, you should look for one with adjustable shelves to accommodate different packages.

It is also important to check the equipment's warranty before purchasing it since some manufacturers offer full-service guarantees covering repair and replacement costs. You should also consider the cost of transportation, installation, and other fees associated with buying a vending machine.

COMPANIES THAT PROVIDE SETUP AND RESTOCKING OF VENDING MACHINES

Many companies provide setup and restocking services for vending machines. These include Vending Solutions, VendMachine Services, and ReCarbon. Each of these companies provides a range of services tailored to individual needs.

Vending Solutions offers professional installation and maintenance, product selection advice, remote monitoring and troubleshooting, after-hours servicing, and customer training. They will also provide you with marketing materials to help promote your business.

ReCarbon provides high-quality used vending machines that have been refurbished to meet current safety standards. They offer machine repair and installation services along with preventative maintenance plans that can be tailored to fit the needs of any business.

VendMachine Services is a full-service vending machine provider that offers setup, restocking, and maintenance services. They also provide customer service support, promotional material printing, and inventory tracking services.

Each company has the experience and resources to provide quality, vending services. Consider all of the available options before making a decision.

CHAPTER XVII

ATMS

The average price for using an ATM is $3. Therefore, most money businesses make using ATMs comes from this fee.

Allowing an ATM to be installed at your place of business can result in a commission for your company. In the simplest terms, a commission is a fee imposed on each ATM user.

Owners of businesses rarely get the total charge. Businesses responsible for the ATM's upkeep (cash replenishment, repairs, etc.) typically collect a portion of rental fees.

The company makes money from the surcharge transactions, although the exact proportion can vary. While businesses can profit from ATM usage fees, some entrepreneurs seek alternative revenue streams. For example, displaying ads on automated teller machines is a frequent practice.

Advertisements are being sold to run on the screens installed on top of ATMs by various companies. In turn, this can boost earnings for ATM providers and their locations.

BENEFITS OF AN ATM

Considering installing an ATM at your business, you may anticipate several advantages. For example, if you are a cash-only business, having an ATM on-site enables customers to withdraw cash to pay you for your products or services. In addition, you receive an additional commission. Other advantages include the following:

INCREASED REVENUE:

The commission you earn on each transaction and the new customers who enter your restaurant to use the ATM could improve your revenue.

REDUCED CREDIT CARD PROCESSING FEES:

Businesses with onsite ATMs receive more cash transactions than those without. Therefore, you can save on credit card processing costs by installing an ATM at your store.

CONVENIENCE:

Providing customers with a simple cash alternative within your organization is a form of customer service. In addition, it could increase customer satisfaction.

FLEXIBLE PLANS:

Depending on what's ideal for your business, ATM vendors frequently offer the option to either purchase or lease a machine. In addition, there are short-term contracts and cancel-at-any-time alternatives. Some companies even offer assistance with ATM marketing.

STARTING AN ATM BUSINESS

Many small business owners may desire to add an ATM to one or more of their sites; if you're planning to create an entity that buys and sells ATMs to small companies, you should be aware of the following factors.

First, as you would before undertaking any commercial activity, conduct market research, including the size of the market, the major players, and how you would finance your organization.

In addition to the factors above, below is a list of standard measures to take when starting your ATM business:

CONSIDER THE STARTUP COSTS

Initial startup costs includes office space, ATM purchases, legal or business formation fees, and staffing expenses.

MAKE A LIST OF RETAIL LOCATIONS WELL SUITED FOR AN ATM

Included in this category are gas stations, bars, and convenience stores. These sites should provide access to your target market.

SELL OR LEASE ATMS TO INTERESTED BUSINESS OWNERS.

When speaking with shops and small business owners, negotiate the best possible bargain while keeping your costs in mind, primarily if you offer a full-service solution.

INSTALL THE ATM

Once the machine has been installed, load it with cash and collect fees. If you are employing a full-service model, you must service the ATM regularly to ensure it is entirely functional.

GROW YOUR BUSINESS

Expand your business by identifying new sites and installing ATMs in them. In proportion to the expansion of your clientele, your employees and ATM stock will also expand.

REQUIREMENTS FOR QUALIFYING TO GET INTO THE ATM BUSINESS

To qualify for an ATM business, an individual must first meet a few requirements.

The individual must be able to demonstrate a sound understanding of the industry's regulations and laws, as well as the ability to abide by them. Most ATM companies require that their clients have at least a basic understanding of the banking industry and its current regulations to do business with them.

The individual should also possess excellent customer service skills and problem-solving capabilities. An ATM owner/operator must be prepared to handle any customer inquiries, troubleshoot technical issues, and resolve complaints quickly and professionally. Additionally, they should also have good knowledge of the local market in which they intend to operate. This helps when it comes to identifying potential locations for their ATM machines.

Next, the individual needs to have sufficient capital to invest in purchasing or leasing ATMs and setting up locations where they'll be placed. These machines can range from several hundred dollars to tens of thousands depending on various factors such as size, features, brand name, etc. Establishing sites is also an expensive endeavour. This entails paying fees for permits and other associated costs such as installation or marketing material production costs.

Finally, an aspiring ATM owner-operator needs adequate insurance coverage for their business operations in case something goes wrong (e.g., theft or vandalism). This safeguards their investments in the event of any losses incurred due to unforeseen circumstances.

IS IT BASED ON CREDITWORTHINESS OR LEGAL BACKGROUND CHECKS AT ALL?

No, it is not based on creditworthiness or legal background checks. To qualify for an ATM business, an individual must meet the abovementioned criteria. This includes understanding the industry's regulations and laws, possessing customer service skills, having sufficient capital to invest in ATMs and sites, and acquiring appropriate insurance coverage.

One ATM vendor is NCR Corporation. NCR Corporation is a global leader in providing technology solutions, including ATMs, to financial and retail institutions worldwide. For over 130 years, they have been creating innovative solutions that help businesses drive customer satisfaction and loyalty. They offer a wide range of ATM models to meet any budget or business need, from compact countertop models to full-service teller ATMs with touchscreen options and cash dispensers. All ATMs are equipped with advanced security features such as EMV chip-and-PIN transactions, encrypted card readers, and comprehensive support services like remote monitoring and management of networked ATMs. In addition, their knowledgeable technical staff can easily configure ATMs for multi-currency or multiple languages.

CHAPTER XVIII

REAL ESTATE

Many people use it to generate a steady income stream, which can then be used to live off of. Of course, real estate investing requires some knowledge and understanding of how the market works and some financial resources to buy or maintain properties. Still, once you get the hang of it, passive income from real estate investments can become your primary source of living.

The process for generating passive income through real estate is fairly simple: you purchase a property (or multiple properties) and rent them out, allowing tenants to pay rent and cover mortgage payments while also giving you extra money in the form of rental payments. In addition, you don't have to deal with day-to-day property management, allowing you to enjoy a steady income stream without much effort.

Real estate can be a great source of passive income that requires consideration and planning. First, you must determine what kind of real estate investment makes sense for your financial situation and consider factors such as location, condition, taxes, and maintenance costs. More importantly, it is essential to understand the legal aspect of owning rental properties to avoid potential problems down the line.

Once you have considered all, you can begin looking at different properties and figuring out how they could generate passive income.

But, again, researching local markets and staying up-to-date with changes in the industry will go a long way in achieving success with real estate investing.

When done correctly, real estate can serve as a great source of passive income that can help you achieve financial freedom and provide the necessary tools to live off your investments. Of course, it will require patience, research, and dedication – but in the end, it could be well worth the effort.

REAL ESTATE INVESTMENT TRUSTS

A real estate investment trust (REIT) is an entity, which owns, manages, or finances real estate that generates revenue.

REITs are similar to mutual funds in that they pool the capital of several participants. This enables private investors to get profits from real estate investments without having to purchase, manage, or finance properties themselves.

REITs offer a great way to gain passive income by taking advantage of the real estate market without getting involved in day-to-day management. Investors can purchase shares of a REIT and receive dividends from the trust's profits, which act as regular income streams. Additionally, investing in REITs can provide capital appreciation when the value of its portfolio increases over time.

Investors interested in this passive income type should research different REITs in order to determine which fits their goals and financial circumstance best. Several types of REITs are available with varying levels of risk, so it is important to do your due diligence before investing. Investors should know the tax implications of owning REITs and consult a tax advisor for more information.

REITs offer an attractive way to invest passively in real estate and generate regular income from rental properties without managing day-to-day operations. Of course, investing in REITs requires research and understanding the risks, but it can be a great source of passive income for those looking to diversify their investments.

THREE TYPES OF REITS EXIST:

- Equity-based REITs. Most REITs are equity REITs, which own and operate real estate earning income. Rents are the primary source of revenue (not by reselling properties).

- Mortgage REITs. These type REITs lend money to real estate owners and operators through mortgages and loans or indirectly through purchasing mortgage-backed securities. Their primary source of income is the net interest margin, which is the difference between the interest they make on home loans and the cost of funding these loans. This model makes them susceptible to an increase in interest rates.

- Hybrid REITs. This particular type REIT uses both equity and mortgage investment strategies.

RENTAL PROPERTY INVESTMENT

Investing in rental property is an excellent way to create passive income. You can earn money from tenants by purchasing and managing rental properties while potentially increasing your property's value over time.

When investing in rental property, it is important to consider location, condition, taxes, and maintenance costs to determine the best investment opportunity. Understanding the legal aspects of owning rental properties is essential to ensure that you are protected and avoid potential problems.

All things considered, you can begin researching different properties to determine how they could generate passive income. Nevertheless, researching local markets and staying abreast of changes in the industry can help you make informed decisions and find the best possible investments.

The fact remains; investing in rental properties can be a remarkable way to establish passive income. Still, it is essential to understand all of the associated risks before taking the plunge. Moreover, with proper planning and management, rental property investments can provide a stable source of income over time.

AIRBNB

Airbnb is another lucrative way to generate passive income. By renting out your home or a room in your home to guests, you can earn money regularly while also taking advantage of the increasing popularity of the "sharing economy." Airbnb does require some work, as you would need to create a profile for your space, communicate with guests, and manage bookings. However, once this is set up, it can be pretty passive with minimal ongoing effort required of you. Airbnb has several resources to help you get started, such as its host guide, a global network of support teams, and even a home-sharing insurance program. With Airbnb's easy-to-use platform and wide selection of properties, it's no wonder why it's quickly become one of the most popular ways to generate passive income.

Before listing your property on Airbnb, there are several things to consider, including researching local laws and regulations, setting up the right insurance policies, assessing safety concerns, and more. Equally as important, it is essential to be aware of any taxes applicable when earning money from hosting on Airbnb.

Once you have researched these details and taken all necessary precautions, you can begin listing your property for rent on Airbnb. First, you must create an attractive listing with photos and helpful information for potential guests. You can also create rules and policies to ensure everything runs smoothly and that you are treated fairly as a host.

VIRTUAL OFFICE SPACE

Renting out virtual office space is yet, another unique but rewarding way to earn passive income. You can earn regular income from tenants who use the space for their business needs. Ideally, you can find potential tenants by advertising your space on websites like WeWork or by reaching out to local businesses.

The amount of money you make depends on the size and location of your space. Since virtual offices are often rented out for short-term contracts, you will likely have a consistent turnover in tenants, which means more opportunities to bring in new income.

While renting out virtual office space may not initially provide a largely passive income stream, it can be a great way to start building up your finances over time if appropriately managed. Inevitably, having additional sources of income could help offset the cost of owning and maintaining a space, making it easier to generate profits in the long run.

CHAPTER XVIIII

ANGEL INVESTING

Angel investing is an increasingly popular method of building passive income. It involves investing in a company before it goes public and has the potential to bring large returns with only a small amount of upfront capital. Angel investors typically receive shares in exchange for their investment, which can provide them with a steady income stream as the company grows and expands. Additionally, angel investors can access other benefits, such as discounts on products or services offered by the companies they invest in.

When done correctly, angel investing can be an excellent source of passive income for those looking to build wealth over time. To become an angel investor, you must know business and finance and understand the legalities surrounding investments. Still, anyone can learn the basics to become a successful angel investor. Many online resources are available to aid in the process of understanding the fundamentals of such.

An angel investor is ordinarily a wealthy person who finances businesses and entrepreneurs in exchange for a stake in the company. Angel investors are also private investors, seed investors, and angel funders. Many times, an entrepreneur will find angel investors within their network. These type investors can contribute either a lump sum to get a company off the ground or a steady stream of capital to see it through its formative years.

Angel investors are private individuals that put money into emerging businesses. They rarely allocate more than 10 percent of their capital to high-risk investments. Most angel investors have a surplus of cash and seek a better return than in more conventional investment vehicles.

Since angel investors typically put their money into the person behind the startup rather than the business itself, they can offer more generous conditions than traditional lenders. Angel investors care more about assisting businesses in their early stages than making a profit for themselves. They function as the antithesis of venture capitalists.

Commonly referred to as informal investors, angel funders, private investors, seed investors, and business angels; they are typically wealthy people who provide the initial business funding in exchange for a stake in the company or convertible debt. Some angel investors use Internet crowdfunding platforms to combine their resources or form angel investor networks.

Angel investments can be hazardous, so it is essential to thoroughly research potential investors and the companies they are investing in. It is equally as important to understand the terms of the investment before entering into any agreement. Despite the risks, angel investments can be an excellent way for entrepreneurs to acquire additional capital and resources for their business ventures.

CHAPTER XX

DIVIDEND STOCKS

Dividends are periodic cash distributions made by a firm to its stockholders. Investors favor dividend stocks because of the high quality and stability of the companies that provide them. Although high dividend companies may seem like a safe bet, investors should proceed with caution because many of these stocks have unusual company structures that could prove to be dangerous. Consider the dividend payout ratio and other indicators of dividend growth (the percent of profits paid to shareholders).

Dividend stocks usually pay out quarterly or semi-annually as a percentage of their overall price. When you purchase shares in dividend stocks, you become eligible to receive a portion of the company's profits as dividends. As such, it is essential to research the company before investing and ensure it is reliable and stable. Buying individual stock can be risky if you don't know enough about the company or sector. To reduce risk when investing in dividend stocks, many investors diversify their portfolios by purchasing several types of stocks from multiple companies within a specific sector or industry. This will help reduce the risk of portfolio loss if one of the stocks performs poorly.

Dividend stocks can be a great way to generate passive income, as they provide a regular flow of income for which you don't have to work actively. Additionally, many dividend stocks offer great long-term potential that can help increase your overall return on investment (ROI). However, it is essential to remember that dividends are not guaranteed and can vary from quarter to quarter or year over year, depending on the company's performance. Therefore, it is essential to understand the risks associated with investing in dividend stocks before taking the plunge. More importantly, you should consult with a financial advisor when making major investment decisions.

CHAPTER XXI

COMPOUND INTEREST INVESTMENTS

Compound interest investments are one of the most reliable, passive income sources. Investing in stocks, mutual funds, and bonds can generate passive income through the return on your investment (ROI). With compounding interest, your capital will grow at a faster rate than with simple interest. For example, if you invest in a stock that pays a 5% dividend each year and compounds annually, then after 10 years, you will have doubled your money. It would be best if you also considered investing in real estate, as this is another excellent source for generating passive income. Real estate investments such as rental properties or vacation homes can give you a steady stream of monthly income from rental payments or sales commissions when sold later. Investing in mutual funds or ETFs (Exchange Traded Funds) can also be a great way to gain passive income. These funds are composed of a basket of stocks, so you'll have multiple sources of dividend payments at different times throughout the year. Lastly, you might consider investing in bonds as they typically pay higher interest rates than traditional savings accounts and other investments. You can use these passive income streams to supplement your regular salary or retirement plans, giving you more financial freedom.

To maximize your returns on compound interest investments, it's important to diversify your portfolio and take advantage of tax-advantaged accounts like IRAs or 401(k)s. Diversifying your portfolio with low-cost index funds and ETFs is a great way to increase your ROI over time. Additionally, by investing in tax-advantaged accounts such as an IRA or 401(k), you can reduce your income taxes and maximize the amount of money you earn from your investments.

Interest can be compounded daily, weekly, monthly, or yearly at your discretion. Although, financial instruments often adhere to predefined compounding frequency plans.

In most cases, the daily compounding schedule utilized by banks for savings accounts is the most prevalent. Depending on the kind of account, a CD may compound daily, monthly, or semi-annually, while money market accounts often compound daily. Most financial products, including mortgages, home equity lines of credit, lines of credit for small businesses, and credit card accounts, use a monthly compounding schedule.

The period interest accrues before being added to the principal balance can also vary. For example, a bank may compound interest daily but only credit it to a customer's account, once a month. The interest will start accruing once it is credited to the account, at which point it will be added to the principal and begin to earn interest.

Continually compounding interest, offered by some financial institutions, involves the addition of interest to the principal balance at any given moment. However, unless you deposit and withdraw funds on the same day, it only adds daily compounding interest.

Investors and creditors benefit from interest compounded more frequently. Unfortunately, the inverse is true for a borrower.

CHAPTER XXII

PASSIVELY INVESTS IN THE MARKETS

Passively investing in the stock market is another fantastic way to gain passive income, hands down. It doesn't require a lot of time or money, and there are many different ways to do it, such as through index funds, ETFs (exchange-traded funds), mutual funds, dividend stocks, and REITs (real estate investment trusts). With the right strategy and research, you could potentially build a steady stream of passive income from your investments.

The key to success with passively investing in the markets is understanding how much risk you can afford to take on, being diligent about researching potential investments before committing any money to them, setting up automatic reinvestment plans for dividends or other returns that come from your investments, and diversifying your investments across multiple different asset classes.

By consistently reinvesting the profits from your investments, you can compound your gains and create a more reliable source of passive income. In addition, actively managing and watching the markets can help you identify potential opportunities or risks that could affect your investments. With enough time and effort, passively investing in the stock market could serves as an effective way to generate long-term passive income.

CHAPTER XXIII

HIGH-YIELD SAVINGS ACCOUNTS

High-yield savings accounts are a popular way to secure passive income, especially if you're unsure about investing in the stock market. High-yield savings accounts offer competitive interest rates and can be opened with little or no money upfront. You may not make a fortune from this passive income, but it's an excellent way to build wealth without putting yourself at too much risk. These accounts can help you save for retirement and other long-term goals. There are even some online banks that will let you open an account with no minimum balance requirements. Investing in a high-yield savings account means making small amounts of passive income in no time.

With high-yield savings accounts, you can earn interest rates of more than the national average.

Ordinarily, people conveniently keep their savings and checking accounts at the same financial institution. However, competition on savings rates has risen, establishing a new category of "high-yield savings accounts," thanks to the rise of internet-only banks and traditional banks that have opened their doors to people across the country via online account opening.

High-yield savings accounts offer a big earnings boost compared to the national average savings rate. For example, if the average annual-percentage yields on savings accounts sums at 0.10% a person with $5,000 in savings would earn only $5 after a year. Alternatively, you could earn $100 by putting the same $5,000 into an account that pays 2%.

Earning much more may necessitate splitting your finances across two banks. Although it may feel strange at first if you're used to having both accounts at the same financial institution, the ease and speed with which electronic transfers can be made between financial institutions today makes it possible to move money between your checking account at Bank A. Likewise, your savings account at Bank B with little effort on your part.

High-yield savings account providers may also have fewer features or fewer products available than traditional banks, making it more challenging to manage all of your financial needs in one place.

You should always verify if a financial institution is a member of the FDIC or NCUA before deciding to open an account there.

You'll also notice that the federal restriction limiting withdrawals from a savings account to six per monthly cycle will affect any bank savings account, whether a regular or a high-yield account.

In light of this information, it is important to learn where and how to open a high-yield account and evaluate whether such an account would be an excellent addition to your existing financial holdings.

MAKING A PLAN FOR YOUR HIGH-INTEREST SAVINGS ACCOUNT

A high-yield savings account is just one component of a well-rounded financial plan. To decide how much cash you should keep liquid, consider how you'll use the account in conjunction with your other savings and investing methods.

For instance, should the savings account act as an emergency fund? Financial experts normally recommend having three to six months of living expenses.

Instead, you're utilizing a high-yield account to save up for a substantial purchase, such as a house, a car, or a big vacation, which you'll make within the following five years. Not investing in things that go down in value during that period is a good idea. So, you can preserve your initial investment and use the interest you earn toward your savings goal if you habitually put money into high-interest savings account regularly.

Others will open a high-yield savings account to hold any extra money after paying bills and covering living expenses. Since the interest rate on a checking account is typically very low if not nothing, transferring overflow funds into savings when they aren't needed for day-to-day transactions can result in a monthly interest payout.

You can utilize more than one of these strategies to partition your savings for many purposes. For example, you can open multiple savings accounts at several banks, and many even allow you to give each account a unique name. Alternatively, you can create high-yield savings accounts at numerous high-interest banks. Having separate savings accounts for various purposes might make it much less hassle to refrain from touching funds you don't want to, like an emergency fund.

WHAT TO LOOK FOR IN A HIGH-YIELD SAVINGS ACCOUNT

Whether you're looking to switch banks or already have access to a high-yield account at your current financial institution, it's always a good idea to shop around and see what other institutions offer. A significant savings amount is particularly susceptible to the cumulative effects of slight differences in interest rates and fees over time. Here are some things to compare:

1. INTEREST RATE

What is the interest rate on the account right now? Is this a permanent rate or a limited-time offer? The interest rates on savings accounts are usually variable and subject to change. It's important to note that the introductory rate offered by some accounts is often valid for a limited time only. Also, see if the advertised rate has any associated minimum or maximum balance requirements.

2. REQUIRED INITIAL DEPOSIT

What is the minimum opening deposit, and can you make that initial commitment?

3. MINIMUM BALANCE REQUIRED

In the future, what minimum balance must be maintained in the account? It's essential to feel confident that you'll always stay within the minimal requirement, otherwise, it could result in penalties or cause the interest rate you were expecting to be cancelled.

4. FEES

Are there any monthly or annual fees associated with this account at the bank or credit union? If so, how can you prevent it (besides ensuring your balance is always over the required minimum)? What is the bank's cost for exceeding the nationally mandated limit of six-monthly withdrawals?

5. LINKS TO OTHER BANKS AND BROKERAGE ACCOUNTS

Does the financial institution permit you to link your high-yield savings account with deposit accounts held at other financial institutions, such as banks or brokerages? Is there a limit to the number of accounts you may connect?

6. ACCESSING YOUR MONEY

If there are other withdrawal methods, what are they? Is an ATM card acceptable for making withdrawals from savings accounts?

7. DEPOSIT OPTIONS

Is there a mobile check deposit app for your smartphone if you plan on depositing checks into your account? If not, can you only use an ATM to deposit your checks?

8. COMPOUNDING METHOD

The interest compounding frequency is negotiable between the bank and the borrower (daily, monthly, quarterly, semi-annually, or annually). Therefore, if you compare accounts using APY rather than the annual interest rate, the compounding component will already be considered, even if more frequent compounding will raise your take-home yield.

CHAPTER XXIIII

LIFE INSURANCE

Life insurance is a type of insurance policy that pays out a lump sum to your family in the event of your death. It can provide financial security for your dependents and help them maintain their lifestyle if something happens to you. With life insurance, you pay an annual premium and receive a lump sum upon passing away. This can be used for funeral costs, medical bills, current or upcoming debts, or any other expenses incurred due to your death.

Many life insurance policies are available, including term and whole life insurance. Depending on the type of policy you choose, there may also be riders that can add additional benefits such as disability income protection or critical illness coverage. When choosing the right life insurance policy for you, it is essential to consider your individual needs and goals.

Life insurance can provide a great source of passive income for you and your family, as the proceeds from the policy can be used in many ways. Depending on the type of policy you choose, life insurance can help support loved ones by providing a lump sum to cover any debts or expenses incurred as a result of your death. It can also be used to fund retirement plans, pay off mortgages, or provide an additional form of income for your dependents.

WHOLE LIFE POLICY

Whole life insurance is a type of permanent life insurance that provides coverage for your entire lifetime. This policy has many benefits, including the ability to build cash value over time, which can be used as an additional source of income or retirement savings.

Whole-life policies are generally more expensive than other life insurance types, but they have some advantages. For example, whole-life policies guarantee a minimum death benefit and provide cash value that will accumulate interest over time. This means that you will receive the death benefit regardless of how long you live, and you can use the cash value from the policy, if needed. This is essential and can be beneficial when building wealth. Additionally, whole-life policies typically come with higher premiums due to their longer-term nature, making them an excellent option for long-term financial security.

Whole-life policies can provide a great source of passive income for you and your family. The cash value from the policy can be used to pay off debts, fund retirement plans, or provide an additional form of income for your dependents. More importantly, whole life insurance benefits are generally tax-free and non-taxable, meaning that any proceeds received upon passing away will not be subject to federal or state taxes.

For those looking for long-term financial security and peace of mind, whole-life insurance is an excellent choice as it provides numerous benefits, including guaranteed death benefits and cash value accumulation over time. So, whether you are looking to create a passive income stream or want the assurance that your loved ones will be taken care of in the event of an untimely death, whole-life insurance is a great option.

TERM LIFE POLICY

Term life insurance is temporary life insurance that provides coverage for a specific amount of time, usually between one and 30 years. This type of policy is often chosen by those who need coverage for a short period, such as when they are raising children or paying off debts. Term life policies generally have lower premiums than permanent policies due to their shorter-term nature, making them more affordable for families on a budget.

Term life policies can provide financial security for you and your family in the event of an untimely death. Still, they typically do not provide the same benefits as permanent policies, such as cash value accumulation and guaranteed death benefits. However, they can be an excellent option for those on a budget or who only need temporary coverage.

Term life insurance is an excellent option if you want to create an additional source of income while also providing financial security for your family. The proceeds from the policy can be used to pay off mortgages, fund retirement plans, or provide an additional form of income for dependents in the event of your passing. Additionally, term life insurance policies typically offer tax-free death benefits, which can help make them even more attractive.

INDEX UNIVERSAL LIFE POLICY

Index Universal Life (IUL) is a permanent life insurance policy that provides death benefits and cash value accumulation over time. This type of policy is often chosen by those looking for more long-term financial security as it offers several unique benefits to its policyholders.

The primary benefit of IUL policies is the potential for cash value accumulation through indexed interest rates linked to an external index such as the S&P 500 or Nasdaq Composite. For example, if the index increases in value, so will your policy's cash value. IUL policies are generally tax-free and non-taxable, making them a rewarding option for those who desire to create a passive income stream or fund retirement plans.

Index Universal Life policies can provide a great source of passive income while offering long-term financial security for you and your family. The cash value from the policy can be used to pay off debts, fund retirement plans, or provide an additional source of income for dependents in the event of an untimely death. In addition, IUL policies have no expiration date, so they will remain in force as long as premiums are paid, and the account is maintained correctly.

Whether you're looking for short-term coverage with a term life policy or long-term financial security with an IUL policy, several options are available for creating a passive income stream. Whole life insurance provides guaranteed death benefits, cash value accumulation, and added peace of mind for you and your family. Index Universal Life policies can also provide a great source of passive income with potential tax savings.

No matter which type of policy you choose, life insurance can be an intelligent way to create an additional source of income while also providing financial security for your loved ones in the event of an untimely death. In addition, investing in life insurance today can provide long-term financial stability and peace of mind for years to come.

CHAPTER XXV

CREATE AN APP

The market value for revenues generated through mobile app downloads is expected to average $935 billion in 2023. Many people who want to become digital nomads believe app development is the key to leaving the 9-to-5 behind for good.

The best benefit is that you need to learn how to code to create an app. After that, all you need is a concept, a design, and marketing to get your app out there.

Whether you create your app or hire a development team (which can be expensive) is up to you. However, plenty of online resources will help with the process.

Once your app is developed, it's just a matter of utilizing the best monetization methods. For example, you can charge users an initial fee for downloading the app, use in-app purchases or ads, or offer subscription services for those who want continued access to features and updates.

It may take several months before your app starts earning money, but if done right and marketed well, you could have passive income rolling in quickly!

HOW YOU CAN BUILD AN APP

FIND A LOW-COMPETITION NICHE

Before diving into app development, you first need to identify a niche. There are millions of apps in the App Store, so finding an area with low competition is important. You can do this by searching for similar apps and seeing how many downloads they're getting and their ratings. Also, make sure you choose something that will appeal to a wide range of users; otherwise, your app won't be successful.

DESIGN AN ATTRACTIVE INTERFACE

Once you have decided on a niche for your app, it's time to design its user interface. Again, you don't need to be a graphic designer or coder to create an attractive and intuitive interface; plenty of online tools are available. In addition, numerous tutorials will walk you through the process.

ADD FEATURES THAT OUTDO THE COMPETITION

To stand out from the competition, you need to add features that your competitors haven't thought of yet. These features should be helpful and add value for users; otherwise, they won't bother using them. Once you have some ideas, you can begin developing the app.

TEST AND REFINE

Before launching an app to the public, it's vital that you test it thoroughly. Create a group of beta testers who will try out the app and provide feedback on what works and doesn't. You may need to make several iterations of your design before it is ready for launch.

HAVE CHEAP OR FREE MARKETING TACTICS READY TO GO.

Once your app is ready, you must get the word out there. Develop a marketing strategy that targets your desired audience and identify cheap or free tactics such as social media posts or influencer endorsements that can help you reach a wider audience. You can also use paid advertising to get more downloads of your app.

KEEP YOUR APP SIMPLE (AT LEAST FOR VERSION ONE)

Keep your app simple. If you're starting, it's better to focus on refining one feature and adding more features in later versions of the app. This will make it easier for users to learn how to use the app quickly and will help improve user retention rates.

BE SMART WITH YOUR REVENUE MODEL

Once your app is launched, you must decide how to monetize it. There are a few options, such as charging a fee for downloading the app, using in-app purchases or ads, or offering subscription services. The most important thing is to choose a model that will generate revenue without annoying users.

OPTIMIZE YOUR APP REGULARLY

Keep an eye on user feedback and optimize your app regularly. This will ensure that your app remains competitive and keeps users happy. Don't be afraid to try new things; sometimes, a small change can make a big difference in engagement and revenue.

CONSIDER AVOIDING GOOGLE PLAY UNTIL YOUR APP HAS PROVEN DEMAND.

Google Play is a great way to reach a wider audience, but it can also be expensive. Focusing on the App Store first and ensuring your app is successful before investing in Google Play is best. This will help you ensure that your investment pays off and that you don't waste money on an unproven product.

DON'T FORGET ABOUT CUSTOMER SERVICE

Finally, customer service is important. Make sure you have someone available to answer user questions and address any issues they may have with the app. This will help keep users happy and promote long-term engagement with your product.

Building an app from scratch is no easy feat, but if you're willing to work and use the right strategies, you can potentially generate significant passive income. The key is to find a low-competition niche, create an attractive user interface, add features that outdo the competition, have cheap or free marketing tactics ready to go, keep your app simple (at least for version one), be smart with your revenue model and optimize your app regularly. Then, with patience and hard work, you can turn your app into a reliable source of income.

Conclusion

Congratulations on making it to the end of this book! I hope you've learned a lot about generating passive income and have found some valuable strategies that you can use to start your journey toward financial freedom.

There are many ways that you can earn passive income. For example, you can start a YouTube channel, become an affiliate marketer, sell digital content like courses or membership websites, write and sell fiction or non-fiction books, create low-content books like organizers or planners, publish magazines digitally or in print, work as a social media influencer, start a blog or buy an existing one, distribute music, and more. You can achieve financial freedom simply by implementing use of the right tools and resources.

Passive income takes time and effort to build up, but it can be lucrative and gratifying if you're willing to do the work. Keep in mind that multiple passive income streams are ideal for heightened success and financial stability, so consider diversifying your sources. The results could be game changing.

Made in the USA
Columbia, SC
07 August 2024